SMART MONEY HABITS FOR TEENS

A Beginner's Guide to Financial Success

PARKER MILES

TABLE OF CONTENTS

INTRODUCTION

Developing good financial habits early in life is one of the most important things a person can do to set themselves up for long-term economic success and stability. The habits and mindsets we form around money in our youth and early adulthood tend to stick with us throughout our lives, so establishing positive patterns from the start can have an enormous positive impact. Conversely, falling into poor financial habits early on can lead to persistent struggles for decades. By cultivating intelligent money management skills and a responsible approach to personal finance from a young age, individuals give themselves a significant advantage in achieving their financial goals and building wealth over time. One of the key benefits of developing good financial habits early is that it allows you to harness the power of compound interest over a longer time horizon. When you start saving and investing at a young age, even small contributions can grow into large sums over the decades, thanks to compound returns. For example, if you start investing $200 per month at age 25 and earn an average 7% annual return, by age 65, you would have over $525,000. But if you wait until age 35 to start that same $200 monthly investment, by 65, you would only have about $245,000 - less than half as much. The earlier you begin, the more time your money has to grow exponentially.

Another crucial financial skill is developing the habit of living below your means and avoiding unnecessary debt from a young age. By learning to distinguish between needs and wants, creating and sticking to a budget, and avoiding trying to keep up with others' spending, you set yourself up to build wealth rather than constantly struggling to make ends meet. When you consistently spend less than you earn and save/invest the difference, you create a virtuous cycle that compounds over time. You can build an emergency fund, save for primary goals like buying a home, and steadily increase your net worth year after year. Good financial habits formed early also help protect you from common money pitfalls that derail many people's finances. For instance, paying off credit card balances in full each month enables you to avoid falling into high-interest credit card debt that can take years to climb out of. Learning to compare, shop, negotiate, and seek out the best deals helps you avoid overpaying for significant purchases. And cultivating the discipline to live on less than you make, even as your income grows, prevents lifestyle inflation from eating up all your earnings gains.

Another key advantage of developing sound money management skills early is that they reduce financial stress and anxiety throughout life. When you have good habits in place—maintaining an emergency fund, living within your means, and saving consistently for the future—you gain a sense of control and security around your finances. You're better equipped to handle unexpected expenses or setbacks without them turning into crises. This peace of mind allows you to focus more energy on other important areas of your life rather than constantly worrying about money. Learning about investing and beginning to invest early is another crucial financial habit that pays significant dividends over time. The sooner you start educating yourself about different investment vehicles, asset allocation, risk management, and long-term investing strategies, the more knowledgeable and comfortable you will make investment decisions. And thanks to the power of compound returns, even small amounts invested in your teens and 20s can grow into significant sums by retirement age. Developing the habit of "paying yourself first" by automatically investing a portion of each paycheck trains you to prioritize your long-term financial health.

Good money habits formed early also help you build a strong credit history and score over time. By consistently paying bills on time, keeping credit card balances low, and responsibly managing different types of credit accounts, you steadily improve your creditworthiness year after year. This translates into better interest rates on mortgages, car loans, and other forms of credit, potentially saving you tens of thousands of dollars over your lifetime. A strong credit score gives you more financial options and flexibility when opportunities arise. Cultivating financial literacy from a young age is another crucial habit that pays off immensely over time. You can make smarter money decisions throughout your life by educating yourself about personal finance topics like budgeting, saving, investing, insurance, taxes, and retirement planning. You're better equipped to evaluate financial products and services, spot potential scams or pitfalls, and optimize your monetary strategy. This knowledge compounds over the years as you apply it to an ever-wider range of financial situations and decisions.

Developing the habit of setting clear financial goals and creating plans to achieve them is another vital money skill to cultivate early. When you get in the practice of defining specific, measurable financial objectives - whether it's saving for a house down payment, building a six-month emergency fund, or maxing out retirement accounts - you give yourself targets to work towards. Creating detailed plans with concrete action steps to reach those goals further increases your odds of success. This goal-setting habit helps you stay focused and motivated in your financial journey over the long term.

Another critical financial habit to establish early is diligently tracking your income and expenses. You gain invaluable insights into your financial patterns and behaviors by keeping careful records of where your money is coming from and where it's going. This data allows you to identify areas where you may be overspending, find opportunities to cut costs, and ensure you're allocating your resources per your priorities and goals. Regularly reviewing your finances also helps you catch errors or fraudulent charges quickly. Developing a long-term perspective on money matters is another crucial financial mindset to cultivate from a young age. By thinking beyond your immediate wants and needs to consider your future financial well-being, you make better decisions in the present. This might mean preceding short-term luxuries or indulgences to save and invest for long-term goals. It also involves considering the opportunity costs of financial choices and evaluating trade-offs between present and future benefits. This forward-thinking approach pays significant dividends over time.

Getting in the habit of continuing to educate yourself about personal finance throughout your life is another key practice to start early. The world of money and investing constantly evolves, with new products, technologies, regulations, and strategies constantly emerging. By cultivating a lifelong learning mindset around financial topics - whether through books, podcasts, courses, or working with advisors - you stay abreast of changes and opportunities that can benefit your financial life. This ongoing education allows you to refine and optimize your approach over time. Learning to communicate openly and honestly about money with partners, family members, and others is another important financial habit to develop early. Many people grow up with a sense of secrecy or shame around financial matters, but this often leads to misunderstandings, conflicts, and poor collective decision-making. By practicing transparency and clear communication about money from a young age, you set the stage for healthier financial relationships. This is especially crucial when it comes to romantic partnerships, as financial issues are a leading cause of relationship stress and divorce.

Cultivating a giving mindset and the habit of charitable donations is another financial practice that pays both personal and societal dividends when started early. Setting aside even small amounts for causes you care about helps you maintain perspective on your finances and connects you to the broader community. Over time, as your means grow, your capacity for impactful giving also expands. Many people find that incorporating philanthropy into their financial lives adds meaning and satisfaction beyond just accumulating wealth for themselves. Another key practice to start early is regularly reviewing and adjusting your financial plan. Your financial needs, goals, and circumstances will inevitably change over time, so it's important to periodically assess your overall strategy. This might involve rebalancing investment portfolios, updating insurance coverage, revising savings targets, or shifting priorities as you move through different life stages. Making this review process a consistent habit ensures your financial approach remains optimally aligned with your evolving situation.

Learning to be patient and avoid impulsive financial decisions is another crucial money habit to cultivate from a young age. In a world of constant marketing messages and pressure to keep up with others, developing the discipline to pause and carefully consider major financial choices is invaluable. This might mean waiting a day or two before making a big purchase to ensure it aligns with your goals and budget. Or it could involve resisting the urge to make drastic changes to your investment strategy based on short-term market fluctuations. This patience and thoughtfulness leads to better outcomes over time. Establishing the habit of maintaining thorough financial records and important documents is another key practice to start early. This includes keeping organized files of tax returns, investment statements, insurance policies, legal documents, and other critical paperwork. Good record-keeping habits make it much easier to manage your finances effectively, prepare accurate tax returns, apply for loans or financial aid, and handle any audits or legal issues that may arise. It also provides peace of mind knowing you can quickly access important information.

Another crucial financial habit to cultivate early is developing a healthy relationship with money and avoiding extreme behaviors or attitudes. This means steering clear of excessive frugality that deprives you of joy and reckless spending that jeopardizes your future. It involves finding a balanced approach that allows you to enjoy life in the present while still planning responsibly for the future. Cultivating this balanced mindset helps you avoid the stress and potential mental health issues that can come from an unhealthy fixation on money.

Learning to advocate for yourself financially - whether negotiating a salary, disputing an erroneous charge, or seeking better terms on a loan - is another key money skill to develop early. Many people, especially women and those from certain cultural backgrounds, are conditioned to avoid confrontation around financial matters. But cultivating the confidence and skills to stand up for your financial interests can have a huge impact over time. Even small wins in negotiations or cost savings add to significant amounts throughout a lifetime.

Another important practice to start young is developing the habit of staying informed about larger economic trends and how they might impact your personal finances. This doesn't mean obsessing over daily stock market moves but rather maintaining a broad awareness of factors like inflation, interest rates, housing market trends, and major policy changes that could affect your financial life. This knowledge allows you to make more informed decisions and potentially adjust your strategy to take advantage of favorable conditions or protect yourself from adverse ones. Finally, cultivating a growth mindset around your financial capabilities is a crucial habit to develop early. Many people believe they're "just not good with money" or that financial success is out of their reach. But money management is a set of learnable skills that anyone can improve with effort and practice. By approaching your financial journey with curiosity, openness to learning from mistakes, and belief in your ability to grow, you set yourself up for continuous improvement and long-term success.

The habits and mindsets we develop around money in our youth and early adulthood impact our long-term financial outcomes. By consciously cultivating positive financial practices from an early age - from consistent saving and investing to ongoing financial education to maintaining a balanced and growth-oriented money mindset - we give ourselves an enormous advantage in building wealth, achieving our goals, and experiencing financial peace of mind. While it's never too late to improve one's financial habits, starting early allows us to fully harness the power of compound interest and compound knowledge over decades. Prioritizing financial literacy and sound money management skills for young people is one of the most impactful investments we can make in their future success and well-being. Financial literacy is a crucial skill that can profoundly shape your future, impacting nearly every aspect of your life. Financial literacy refers to the ability to understand and effectively use various financial skills, including personal financial management, budgeting, and investing. It's about having the knowledge and confidence to make informed decisions about your money, both in the short term and for your long-term financial well-being. In today's complex economic landscape, being financially literate is not just beneficial; it's essential for navigating the myriad financial challenges and opportunities you'll encounter throughout your life.

One of the primary ways financial literacy shapes your future is by empowering you to take control of your finances. When you understand concepts like budgeting, saving, and managing debt, you're better equipped to make daily smart decisions about your money. This knowledge allows you to create and stick to a budget that aligns with your goals and values, ensuring that your spending habits support rather than hinder your financial aspirations. By tracking your income and expenses, you can identify areas where you might overspend and make necessary adjustments. This level of awareness and control over your finances can reduce stress and anxiety about money matters, improving overall mental health and well-being. Financial literacy also plays a crucial role in helping you build and maintain good credit. Understanding how credit works, including factors that influence your credit score and the implications of different types of debt, can have far-reaching effects on your financial future. A good credit score can open doors to better interest rates on loans and credit cards, potentially saving you thousands of dollars over your lifetime. It can also affect your ability to rent an apartment, secure certain jobs, or obtain favorable insurance rates. By grasping the importance of credit and how to manage it responsibly, you set yourself up for greater financial opportunities and flexibility in the future.

Another significant way financial literacy shapes your future is through its impact on your saving and investing habits. When you understand the power of compound interest and the importance of saving early, you're more likely to prioritize putting money aside for both short-term and long-term objectives like retirement. This knowledge can motivate you to start investing at a younger age, giving your money more time to grow and potentially leading to a much larger nest egg by the time you retire. Understanding different investment vehicles, risk tolerance, and the principles of diversification allows you to make informed decisions about allocating your savings to align with your financial goals and risk comfort level. Financial literacy also equips you with the tools to navigate major life decisions more confidently and clearly. Whether you're considering buying a home, starting a business, or planning for a family, a solid foundation in financial literacy helps you assess the financial implications of these choices more effectively. You'll be better prepared to evaluate mortgage options, understand entrepreneurship's financial risks and rewards, or calculate the long-term costs of raising children. This knowledge allows you to make these significant life decisions from a place of informed understanding rather than uncertainty or impulsivity.

In career and professional development, financial literacy can play a pivotal role in shaping your future. Understanding the financial aspects of different career paths, including potential salary trajectories, benefits packages, and the long-term financial implications of various industries, can help guide your career choices. It can also empower you to negotiate salaries and benefits more effectively, ensuring you're fairly compensated for your skills and experience. Moreover, financial literacy can help you make informed decisions about professional development opportunities, weighing the costs of additional education or training against potential future earnings. Financial literacy is also crucial for protecting yourself against fraud and predatory practices. Unfortunately, scams and misleading financial products are common in an increasingly complex financial world. By developing a strong foundation in financial literacy, you're better equipped to recognize red flags, understand the fine print in financial agreements, and make informed decisions about financial products and services. This knowledge can help you avoid costly mistakes and protect your hard-earned money from those seeking to exploit financial ignorance.

Understanding taxes is another vital aspect of financial literacy that can significantly impact your future. Knowledge about different types of taxes, deductions, and credits can help you make strategic decisions to minimize your tax burden legally. This might involve choosing certain investment vehicles, timing major purchases or sales, or structuring your income tax-efficiently. Over a lifetime, a solid understanding of tax principles can lead to substantial savings and more efficient wealth accumulation.

Financial literacy is also crucial in preparing for and navigating unexpected life events. Having a strong financial foundation can make these challenging situations more manageable, whether it's a job loss, medical emergency, or natural disaster. Understanding the importance of emergency funds, insurance coverage, and having a financial contingency plan can provide a safety net during difficult times. This preparation can help weather financial storms without derailing your long-term financial goals. For those considering starting a family, financial literacy becomes even more critical in shaping the future. It helps plan for the costs assessing children, including education expenses, healthcare, and daily living costs. Understanding college savings plans, life insurance, and estate planning becomes crucial for ensuring your family's financial security. Moreover, being financially literate allows you to pass on valuable money management skills to your children, potentially influencing their financial futures. Financial literacy can play a significant role in fostering harmony and avoiding conflicts in relationships. Money is often cited as a major source of relationship tension, particularly in marriages. When both partners are financially literate, they can have more productive conversations about money, set shared financial goals, and work together more effectively to achieve them. This shared understanding can lead to stronger, more stable relationships and a more secure financial future for the family unit.

As you approach retirement age, the impact of financial literacy on your future becomes even more apparent. Understanding retirement account options, Social Security benefits, and strategies for drawing down savings can make the difference between a comfortable retirement and financial struggle in your later years. Financial literacy helps you plan realistically for your retirement needs, make informed decisions about when to retire, and structure your retirement income to last throughout your lifetime. Financial literacy also shapes your ability to leave a lasting legacy. Whether you're interested in philanthropic giving, passing wealth to future generations, or ensuring the financial security of loved ones after you're gone, a strong foundation in financial literacy is essential. It helps you understand estate planning tools, tax-efficient giving strategies, and how to structure inheritances that align with your values and intentions.

Financial literacy can also shape your ability to take advantage of international opportunities in an increasingly globalized world. Understanding concepts like currency exchange, international investing, and the financial implications of living or working abroad can open up a world of possibilities. This knowledge can influence decisions about where to live, work, or retire, potentially leading to a more diverse and enriching life experience. Financial literacy can also play a role in shaping your impact on broader economic and social issues. When you understand how financial systems work, you're better equipped to engage in informed discussions about economic policy, understand the implications of government financial decisions, and make choices as a consumer and investor that align with your values. This might involve making socially responsible investment choices, supporting businesses that align with your ethics, or advocating for financial policies that benefit society. As technology transforms the financial landscape, financial literacy becomes even more critical in shaping your future. Understanding emerging financial technologies like cryptocurrency, blockchain, and digital banking can help you navigate new financial opportunities and risks. It can also help you make informed decisions about adopting new financial tools and services to streamline your financial management or open new investment avenues.

Moreover, financial literacy can shape your future by influencing your overall life satisfaction and sense of security. Feeling confident in your ability to manage your finances and work towards your financial goals can lead to reduced stress, increased peace of mind, and a greater sense of control over your life. This financial confidence can spill over into other areas of your life, potentially leading to more fulfilling personal and professional pursuits. Financial literacy also shapes your resilience in economic downturns or market volatility. When you understand market cycles, the principles of long-term investing, and the importance of diversification, you're less likely to make panic-driven financial decisions during turbulent times. This knowledge can help you stay the course with your long-term financial strategy, potentially avoiding costly mistakes that could derail your financial future.

In conclusion, financial literacy is a powerful tool that can profoundly shape your future in numerous ways. From day-to-day money management to long-term financial planning, from career decisions to retirement preparation, and personal relationships to broader economic engagement, the impact of financial literacy permeates virtually every aspect of life. By investing in your financial education and continuously improving your financial literacy, you're not just acquiring knowledge but actively shaping a future of greater financial security, opportunity, and personal fulfillment. In an increasingly complex financial world, understanding and skillfully navigating financial matters is more than just a useful skill – it's a fundamental pillar of personal empowerment and success. The future you shape through financial literacy is one of informed choices, reduced financial stress, and increased potential for achieving your life goals and dreams.

"Smart Money Habits for Teens: A Beginner's Guide to Financial Success" is a comprehensive and engaging book designed to equip teenagers with essential financial knowledge and skills to set them on the path to long-term financial success. The book is structured to make complex financial concepts accessible and relevant to young readers, gradually building their understanding and confidence in managing money. Through clear explanations, practical examples, and interactive exercises, this guide aims to instill smart money habits that will serve readers well into adulthood. The book begins with an introduction emphasizing the importance of financial literacy for teenagers. It highlights how the habits and knowledge acquired during these formative years can impact one's financial future. This section also outlines the book's objectives and provides an overview of what readers can expect to learn, setting the stage for the following chapters. Readers will find practical exercises and real-life scenarios that help reinforce the concepts discussed throughout the book. These include budgeting worksheets, savings challenges, investment simulations, and case studies of teens successfully managing their finances. The book also features sidebar sections with interesting financial facts, historical anecdotes, and profiles of successful young entrepreneurs and investors.

By reading "Smart Money Habits for Teens: A Beginner's Guide to Financial Success," teenagers will comprehensively understand personal finance tailored to their life stage. They will learn practical skills such as creating and sticking to a budget, setting financial goals, and making informed decisions about spending and saving. The book will help them understand the basics of earning money, including how to find and maintain a part-time job or start a small business. Readers will develop an appreciation for the power of saving and compound interest, learning strategies to make their money grow over time. They'll gain insights into the world of investing, understanding different investment vehicles and the basics of risk management. The book will demystify credit and debt, helping teens understand how to use credit responsibly and avoid common pitfalls that can lead to financial difficulties.

Importantly, the book will equip young readers with the knowledge to navigate the increasingly digital world of finance. They'll learn about online and mobile banking, understanding both these technologies' conveniences and potential risks. The book will also introduce them to various fintech tools that can aid in budgeting, saving, and investing. Readers will gain a basic understanding of taxes, insurance, and other financial concepts that will become increasingly relevant as they enter adulthood. They'll learn to protect their financial information and avoid scams and fraudulent schemes. The book will also foster an understanding of the broader economic landscape, helping teens make connections between personal finance and larger economic trends. Beyond practical skills, the book aims to instill positive financial attitudes and behaviors. Readers will learn the importance of delayed gratification, the value of setting and working towards financial goals, and the benefits of cultivating a giving mindset. They'll develop critical thinking skills that will help them evaluate financial information and make informed decisions.

Perhaps most importantly, "Smart Money Habits for Teens" will empower young readers to take control of their financial futures. The book aims to boost teens' confidence in managing money and making financial decisions by providing a solid foundation in financial literacy. It encourages them to start good financial habits early, leading them to long-term financial success and stability. "Smart Money Habits for Teens: A Beginner's Guide to Financial Success" offers a comprehensive, engaging, and age-appropriate introduction to personal finance. By covering a wide range of topics from basic budgeting to more complex concepts like investing and taxes, the book provides a roadmap for financial literacy that will serve readers well beyond their teenage years. Through its practical approach, interactive elements, and emphasis on developing positive financial habits, this guide aims to equip the next generation with the knowledge and skills they need to navigate the complex financial landscape of the 21st century.

Chapter 1

UNDERSTANDING
MONEY AND HOW IT WORKS

Currency is a fundamental concept in the world of economics and finance, serving as the backbone of modern monetary systems. At its core, currency is a medium of exchange that facilitates trade and economic transactions within a society. It represents a standardized unit of value that people agree to use for buying and selling goods and services. While the concept of currency might seem straightforward, its history, forms, and functions are complex and have evolved significantly over time. The origins of currency can be traced back thousands of years to when early civilizations began to move away from barter systems. In a barter economy, people directly exchanged goods and services for other goods and services. However, this system had significant limitations, such as the difficulty in finding someone who both had what you wanted and wanted what you had to offer. The introduction of currency solved this "double coincidence of wants" problem by providing a universally accepted medium of exchange.

Early forms of currency varied widely across different cultures and regions. Some of the earliest known currencies included cowrie shells, which were used in parts of Africa, Asia, and Oceania. Other early forms included metal tools, beads, and even large stone discs, as seen in the case of Rai stones used on the island of Yap. As societies became more complex, precious metals like gold and silver began to emerge as preferred forms of currency due to their durability, portability, and intrinsic value. The development of coin-based currency marked a significant milestone in the evolution of money. Coins, typically made from precious metals, offered a standardized and easily divisible form of currency. The first known coins were minted in Lydia (modern-day Turkey) around 600 BCE. The use of coins spread rapidly across the ancient world, with various empires and city-states developing their own coinage systems. Paper money, another major innovation in the history of currency, first appeared in China during the Tang Dynasty (618-907 CE). Initially, these were promissory notes issued by merchants, which eventually evolved into government-issued paper currency. The concept of paper money took centuries to gain widespread acceptance in the Western world, with European countries gradually adopting it from the 17th century onwards.

In modern times, currency typically takes two primary forms: physical cash (coins and banknotes) and digital currency. Physical cash remains an important part of many economies, offering a tangible and widely accepted form of payment. Banknotes, the paper bills we commonly use, are typically issued by a country's central bank and feature various security measures to prevent counterfeiting. Digital currency, on the other hand, refers to money that exists only in electronic form. This includes the balances in our bank accounts, which we can access through debit cards, online banking, or mobile payment apps. The rise of digital currency has dramatically changed how we conduct financial transactions, making it possible to transfer money instantly across great distances and facilitating global trade. One of the key characteristics of modern currency is that it is typically fiat money. Fiat currency derives its value not from the material it's made from, but from government decree and public trust. Unlike commodity money (such as gold coins), which has intrinsic value, fiat money is not backed by physical commodities. Instead, its value is based on the stability and creditworthiness of the issuing government.

The value of a currency is influenced by various factors, including the economic strength of the issuing country, inflation rates, interest rates, political stability, and international trade balances. Currency values can fluctuate relative to each other, giving rise to foreign exchange markets where currencies are traded. Each country typically has its own national currency, which serves as legal tender within its borders. Some of the world's major currencies include the U.S. Dollar, Euro, Japanese Yen, British Pound, and Chinese Yuan. These currencies are widely used in international trade and finance, with the U.S. Dollar often serves as a global reserve currency. In some cases, multiple countries may share a common currency. The Euro, for example, is the official currency of 19 of the 27 member states of the European Union. Such currency unions aim to facilitate trade and economic integration among member countries. Currency plays several crucial roles in an economy. Firstly, it serves as a medium of exchange, allowing people to buy and sell goods and services without the need for barter. This greatly increases economic efficiency and facilitates specialization and division of labor. Secondly, currency functions as a unit of account. It provides a common measure of value, allowing us to compare the relative worth of different goods and services. This role of currency is essential for pricing, accounting, and economic calculation. Thirdly, currency acts as a store of value. It allows people to save their earnings for future use, although the effectiveness of this function can be eroded by inflation. The ability to store value is crucial for long-term economic planning and investment. The management of currency is typically the responsibility of a country's central bank. Central banks play a crucial role in monetary policy, controlling the money supply and influencing interest rates to maintain price stability and support economic growth. They also oversee the printing and distribution of physical currency and work to maintain public confidence in the monetary system.

In recent years, the concept of currency has been further expanded with the emergence of cryptocurrencies. These are digital or virtual currencies that use cryptography for security and operate independently of central banks. Bitcoin, introduced in 2009, was the first and remains the most well-known cryptocurrency. While cryptocurrencies have gained significant attention and adoption, they remain a subject of debate regarding their status as "true" currencies. Understanding currency also involves grasping the concept of exchange rates. An exchange rate is the rate at which one currency can be exchanged for another. Exchange rates can be fixed (set by government policy) or floating (determined by supply and demand in foreign exchange markets). Changes in exchange rates can have significant impacts on international trade, tourism, and global economic relations.

The stability of a currency is crucial for economic health. Rapid inflation (a general increase in prices and fall in the purchasing power of money) or deflation (a general decrease in prices and increase in the purchasing power of money) can have severe economic consequences. Central banks work to maintain price stability, often targeting a low, stable inflation rate. Currency also plays a role in a country's sovereignty and national identity. The ability to issue and control a national currency is an important aspect of economic sovereignty. Many countries feature national symbols, historical figures, or cultural landmarks on their banknotes and coins, reflecting their heritage and values. The future of currency is likely to see continued evolution. The trend towards digital payments and cashless societies is accelerating in many parts of the world. Some countries are exploring the concept of Central Bank Digital Currencies (CBDCs), which would be digital forms of fiat money issued by central banks. In conclusion, currency is a fundamental concept that underpins modern economic systems. It serves as a medium of exchange, unit of account, and store of value, facilitating trade and economic activity. From its origins in ancient civilizations to the complex global financial systems of today, currency has constantly evolved to meet the changing needs of societies and economies. Understanding currency – its forms, functions, and the factors that influence its value – is essential for navigating the modern financial world. As we move further into the digital age, the concept of currency continues to evolve, presenting both challenges and opportunities for individuals, businesses, and governments alike. Whether in the form of physical cash, digital balances, or emerging cryptocurrencies, currency remains at the heart of our economic interactions, shaping how we trade, save, and perceive value in our increasingly interconnected world.

The economy is a complex system that governs the production, distribution, and consumption of goods and services within a society. Understanding how the economy works is crucial for individuals, businesses, and policymakers alike. At its core, the economy operates on several fundamental principles, with supply and demand being among the most important. These principles, along with concepts like inflation, economic growth, and market structures, form the foundation of economic theory and practice. Supply and demand are the primary forces that drive market economies. Supply refers to the quantity of a good or service that producers are willing and able to offer at various price points. Demand, on the other hand, represents the quantity of a good or service that consumers are willing and able to purchase at different prices. The interaction between supply and demand determines the market price and quantity of goods and services in an economy.

The law of supply states that, all else being equal, as the price of a good or service increases, the quantity supplied will increase. This is because higher prices incentivize producers to increase production to capture more profits. Conversely, lower prices may lead to a decrease in supply as producers find it less profitable to produce the good or service. The law of demand posits that, all else being equal, as the price of a good or service increases, the quantity demanded will decrease. This is because consumers typically seek to maximize their utility (satisfaction) while minimizing costs. As prices rise, consumers may seek alternatives or reduce their consumption of the good or service. The point at which the supply and demand curves intersect is known as the equilibrium price and quantity. At this point, the quantity supplied equals the quantity demanded, and the market is said to be in equilibrium. If the price is above equilibrium, there will be a surplus of goods, leading to downward pressure on prices. If the price is below equilibrium, there will be a shortage, putting upward pressure on prices. Changes in supply and demand can occur due to various factors. For supply, these might include changes in production costs, technological advancements, or changes in the number of producers. Demand can be affected by factors such as changes in consumer income, preferences, or the prices of related goods (substitutes or complements).

Elasticity is another important concept related to supply and demand. It measures the responsiveness of quantity supplied or demanded to changes in price or other factors. Goods with elastic demand see large changes in quantity demanded in response to price changes, while those with inelastic demand see smaller changes. Understanding elasticity is crucial for businesses in setting prices and for policymakers in predicting the effects of taxes or subsidies. Inflation is another key economic concept that plays a significant role in how the economy works. Inflation refers to a general increase in prices and a corresponding decrease in the purchasing power of money over time. While some level of inflation is generally considered normal and even beneficial for economic growth, high or unpredictable inflation can have severe negative consequences for an economy. There are several types of inflation. Demand-pull inflation occurs when aggregate demand in an economy outpaces aggregate supply, leading to higher prices. Cost-push inflation happens when the costs of production increase, causing businesses to raise prices to maintain profitability. Built-in inflation, also known as wage-price spiral, occurs when workers expect future prices to be higher and demand increased wages, which in turn leads businesses to raise prices to cover higher wage costs. Central banks play a crucial role in managing inflation through monetary policy. They typically aim to maintain a low, stable rate of inflation, often around 2% per year. Tools used to control inflation include adjusting interest rates and managing the money supply. Higher interest rates can help curb inflation by making borrowing more expensive, which can reduce spending and investment. Conversely, lower interest rates can stimulate economic activity but may risk increasing inflation. Economic growth is another fundamental aspect of how the economy works. It refers to an increase in the production of goods and services in an economy over time, typically measured by the growth rate of Gross Domestic Product (GDP). Economic growth is influenced by factors such as technological advancements, increases in productivity, accumulation of capital, and improvements in human capital through education and training.

The business cycle describes the natural fluctuations in economic activity that economies experience over time. It consists of periods of expansion (growth), followed by periods of contraction (recession), and then recovery.

Understanding the business cycle is crucial for businesses and policymakers in making decisions about investment, hiring, and economic policies. Market structures play a significant role in how the economy functions. These structures range from perfect competition, where many small firms compete and no single firm has significant market power, to monopoly, where a single firm dominates the market. In between are structures like monopolistic competition and oligopoly. The type of market structure influences factors such as pricing, production levels, and innovation within industries. Government intervention in the economy is another important aspect of how economies work. Governments can influence economic activity through fiscal policy (government spending and taxation) and regulations. Fiscal policy can be used to stimulate economic growth during recessions or to cool down an overheating economy. Regulations can be implemented to address market failures, protect consumers, or achieve social objectives. International trade and globalization have become increasingly important in understanding how modern economies work. The theory of comparative advantage suggests that countries can benefit by specializing in the production of goods and services in which they have a relative cost advantage and trading with other countries. International trade can lead to increased efficiency, lower prices for consumers, and economic growth. However, it can also lead to job displacement in certain sectors and raise concerns about economic sovereignty. Financial markets play a crucial role in the functioning of modern economies. These markets facilitate the allocation of capital from savers to borrowers and investors. They include stock markets, bond markets, foreign exchange markets, and commodity markets. Financial markets influence economic activity by affecting the cost of borrowing, providing signals about the health of companies and economies, and facilitating investment.

Labor markets are another key component of how economies work. They involve the buying and selling of labor services. Factors such as education levels, skills, labor laws, and technological change all influence the supply and demand for labor. Understanding labor markets is crucial for addressing issues such as unemployment, wage inequality, and the impact of automation on jobs.

Productivity growth is a critical driver of long-term economic growth and improvements in living standards. It refers to the ability to produce more output with the same amount of input. Factors that can increase productivity include technological advancements, improved education and training, better management practices, and more efficient allocation of resources. Economic inequality is an important issue in understanding how economies work and their impact on society. While some level of inequality can provide incentives for innovation and hard work, excessive inequality can lead to social and economic problems. Factors contributing to inequality include differences in education and skills, technological change, globalization, and government policies. Behavioral economics is a field that has gained prominence in recent years, challenging some of the assumptions of traditional economic theory. It incorporates insights from psychology to understand how people actually make economic decisions, often in ways that deviate from purely rational behavior. This has important implications for understanding consumer behavior, financial decision-making, and the effectiveness of economic policies. Externalities are another important concept in economics. These are costs or benefits that affect a third party who did not choose to incur them. Negative externalities, such as pollution, occur when the social cost of an activity exceeds the private cost. Positive externalities, like education, occur when the social benefit exceeds the private benefit. Understanding externalities is crucial for developing policies to address market failures and promote social welfare. The role of information in the economy is also crucial. Perfect information is one of the assumptions of many economic models, but in reality, information asymmetries are common. These asymmetries can lead to market failures and inefficiencies. The field of information economics explores how information affects economic decision-making and market outcomes.

Sustainable development has become an increasingly important consideration in understanding how economies work. This concept emphasizes the need for economic growth that doesn't deplete natural resources or harm the environment in ways that will negatively impact future generations. It involves balancing economic growth with environmental protection and social equity. In conclusion, understanding how the economy works involves grasping a wide range of interconnected concepts and principles. From the fundamental laws of supply and demand to complex issues like inflation, economic growth, and market structures, each aspect plays a crucial role in shaping economic outcomes. The interplay between these various elements creates a dynamic system that influences every aspect of our lives, from individual purchasing decisions to global economic trends. As economies continue to evolve, new challenges and opportunities arise. The digital revolution, climate change, changing demographics, and geopolitical shifts are just some of the factors shaping the future of how economies work. Understanding these fundamental economic principles and their real-world applications is essential for navigating the complexities of modern economic life, whether as consumers, business leaders, or policymakers. By grasping how the economy works, we can make more informed decisions, anticipate economic trends, and contribute to discussions about how to create more prosperous, equitable, and sustainable economic systems for the future.

Personal finance is a crucial life skill that encompasses the management of an individual's financial resources. It involves making informed decisions about earning, spending, saving, investing, and protecting one's money. Understanding personal finance is essential for achieving financial stability, reaching long-term goals, and navigating the complex financial landscape of modern life. At its core, personal finance revolves around three primary components: income, expenses, and the effective management of money. Income is the foundation of personal finance. It represents the money an individual receives, typically through employment, investments, or other sources. Understanding income goes beyond simply knowing how much money one earns. It involves comprehending the various forms of income, such as salary, wages, commissions, bonuses, investment returns, and passive income streams. Each type of income may have different tax implications and potential for growth. For most people, earned income from a job or business is the primary source of funds. This makes career planning and development an integral part of personal finance. Investing in education, skills development, and networking can lead to increased earning potential over time. Additionally, exploring opportunities for promotions, changing careers, or starting a side business can all contribute to income growth. Understanding gross income versus net income is crucial. Gross income is the total amount earned before any deductions, while net income is the amount actually received after taxes and other deductions. Being aware of these differences helps in accurate budgeting and financial planning. Diversifying income sources can provide financial stability and growth opportunities. This might involve developing multiple income streams through investments, rental properties, freelance work, or online businesses. Diversification can help protect against the risk of losing a single income source and can accelerate wealth accumulation. Expenses form the second key component of personal finance. These are the outflows of money for various goods and services. Understanding and managing expenses is crucial for maintaining financial health and achieving financial goals. Expenses can be broadly categorized into fixed expenses (those that remain relatively constant, like rent or mortgage payments) and variable expenses (those that fluctuate, like food or entertainment costs). One of the fundamental principles of sound personal finance is living below one's means – that is, spending less than one earns. This requires careful tracking and management of expenses. Creating a detailed budget is an essential tool for this purpose. A budget helps individuals understand where their money is going and identify areas where spending can be reduced or optimized.

Distinguishing between needs and wants is a crucial skill in managing expenses. Needs are essentials required for basic living, such as food, shelter, and healthcare. Wants are desirable but not necessary items or experiences. Prioritizing needs over wants helps in allocating financial resources more effectively. Awareness of lifestyle inflation is important in managing expenses. As income increases, there's often a tendency to increase spending on lifestyle upgrades. While some lifestyle improvements can enhance quality of life, unchecked lifestyle inflation can prevent individuals from achieving long-term financial goals. Understanding the true cost of purchases is another key aspect of managing expenses. This involves considering not just the initial price of an item, but also ongoing costs, maintenance, and potential depreciation. For example, when buying a car, one should consider not just the purchase price, but also insurance, fuel, maintenance, and depreciation costs. Effective money management is the third pillar of personal finance, bridging the gap between income and expenses. It involves making informed decisions about how to allocate financial resources to meet current needs while also planning for the future. Good money management skills are essential for achieving financial stability and long-term success. One of the fundamental principles of money management is paying yourself first. This means allocating a portion of income to savings and investments before spending on other expenses. This habit helps build wealth over time and provides a financial cushion for emergencies or future goals. Creating and maintaining an emergency fund is a crucial aspect of money management. This fund, typically recommended to cover 3-6 months of living expenses, provides a financial safety net in case of unexpected events like job loss, medical emergencies, or major repairs. Having an emergency fund can prevent the need to rely on high-interest debt in times of crisis. Debt management is another critical component of personal finance. While some forms of debt, like mortgages or student loans, can be considered investments in the future, high-interest consumer debt can be a significant obstacle to financial progress. Understanding different types of debt, their costs, and strategies for repayment is essential. Prioritizing the repayment of high-interest debt while avoiding taking on unnecessary new debt is a key principle of sound financial management.

Saving for short-term and long-term goals is an important aspect of money management. Short-term goals might include saving for a vacation or a down payment on a car, while long-term goals often revolve around retirement planning or funding a child's education. Setting clear, specific financial goals and developing strategies to achieve them is crucial for financial success. Investing is a key component of long-term financial planning. While saving preserves capital, investing allows money to grow over time, potentially outpacing inflation. Understanding different investment options, such as stocks, bonds, mutual funds, and real estate, is important. Equally crucial is understanding concepts like risk tolerance, diversification, and the power of compound interest. Risk management and insurance play vital roles in protecting financial health. This involves identifying potential risks to one's financial well-being and taking steps to mitigate them. Various types of insurance, such as health insurance, life insurance, disability insurance, and property insurance, can provide protection against unforeseen events that could otherwise be financially devastating. Tax planning is another important aspect of personal finance. Understanding how different types of income are taxed, being aware of available deductions and credits, and making strategic decisions to minimize tax liability can significantly impact overall financial health. This might involve strategies like contributing to tax-advantaged retirement accounts or timing investment sales to manage capital gains taxes.

Developing financial literacy is crucial for effective personal finance management. This involves ongoing education about financial concepts, products, and strategies. Staying informed about economic trends, changes in tax laws, and new financial products can help individuals make more informed decisions and adapt their financial strategies as needed. The use of technology in personal finance has become increasingly important. Various apps and online tools are available for budgeting, tracking expenses, managing investments, and monitoring credit scores. Leveraging these tools can make financial management more efficient and provide valuable insights into spending patterns and financial health. Behavioral finance is an important consideration in personal finance. Understanding one's own psychological biases and emotional reactions to financial decisions can help in making more rational choices. Common biases like loss aversion, overconfidence, and present bias can significantly impact financial decision-making. Regular financial check-ups are essential for maintaining financial health. This involves periodically reviewing one's financial situation, reassessing goals, and making adjustments as needed. Life changes such as marriage, having children, changing jobs, or approaching retirement often necessitate updates to financial strategies.

Understanding and managing credit is another crucial aspect of personal finance. A good credit score can lead to better interest rates on loans and credit cards, potentially saving thousands of dollars over time. Regularly checking credit reports, understanding factors that influence credit scores, and practicing responsible credit use are important habits. Estate planning, while often overlooked, is an important component of comprehensive personal finance management. This involves planning for the transfer of assets after death, including creating a will, setting up trusts if appropriate, and designating beneficiaries for various accounts. Proper estate planning can ensure that one's financial legacy is distributed according to their wishes and can minimize tax implications for heirs.

The concept of financial independence is an important goal in personal finance. This typically refers to having sufficient personal wealth to live without having to work actively for basic necessities. Achieving financial independence often requires long-term planning, disciplined saving and investing, and potentially developing passive income streams. Balancing current lifestyle with future financial security is one of the ongoing challenges in personal finance. While it's important to enjoy the present, neglecting future financial needs can lead to difficulties later in life. Finding the right balance requires careful consideration of personal values, goals, and risk tolerance. Adapting to major life transitions is another important aspect of personal finance. Events such as graduating from college, getting married, having children, changing careers, or retiring all have significant financial implications. Being prepared for these transitions and understanding their financial impacts is crucial for maintaining financial stability throughout life's changes. In conclusion, personal finance is a multifaceted field that touches every aspect of our lives. It involves understanding and managing income, controlling expenses, and making informed decisions about how to allocate financial resources. By developing strong personal finance skills, individuals can achieve greater financial stability, reduce stress related to money matters, and work towards achieving their long-term goals and dreams.

Effective personal finance management requires a combination of knowledge, discipline, and adaptability. It's not just about maximizing wealth, but about using financial resources in a way that aligns with personal values and life objectives. Whether it's saving for a home, planning for retirement, funding education, or simply achieving peace of mind, good personal finance practices provide the foundation for a more secure and fulfilling life.

As the financial landscape continues to evolve with new technologies, products, and economic realities, staying informed and continuously educating oneself about personal finance becomes increasingly important. By mastering the basics of income management, expense control, and effective money management, individuals can navigate the complex world of finance with confidence, making informed decisions that support their current needs and future aspirations.

Understanding personal finance is crucial for teenagers as they begin to navigate the world of money management. Many teens have successfully implemented smart financial habits, demonstrating that it's never too early to start building a strong financial foundation. Here are various real-life examples of teenagers managing their money effectively, showcasing different aspects of personal finance. Sarah, a 16-year-old high school student, exemplifies the power of budgeting and saving. After getting her first part-time job at a local café, Sarah decided to create a simple budget to manage her earnings. She allocates 50% of her income to savings, 30% for discretionary spending, and 20% for future educational expenses. By sticking to this budget, Sarah has managed to save $2,000 over the course of a year, which she plans to use for college application fees and textbooks. Her disciplined approach to budgeting has not only helped her save money but also taught her valuable lessons about financial prioritization and delayed gratification. Alex, a 17-year-old aspiring entrepreneur, demonstrates how teens can leverage their skills and interests to generate income. Passionate about graphic design, Alex started creating logos and social media graphics for local small businesses. He charges competitive rates and reinvests a portion of his earnings into online courses to improve his skills. Alex opened a separate business checking account to keep his personal and business finances separate, a smart practice he learned from researching small business management. By treating his design work as a serious business venture, Alex is not only earning money but also gaining valuable entrepreneurial experience that will serve him well in the future.

Emma, a 15-year-old environmentally conscious student, shows how personal values can align with financial decisions. She started a campaign in her school to reduce plastic waste and used her babysitting earnings to purchase a reusable water bottle and lunch containers. Emma also researched ethical and sustainable brands, opting to spend a bit more on clothing and products that align with her values. To afford these choices, she actively looks for ways to reduce expenses in other areas, such as walking or biking instead of asking for rides, which saves on transportation costs. Emma's approach demonstrates how teens can make financial decisions that reflect their personal beliefs and priorities. Marcus, an 18-year-old recent high school graduate, provides an excellent example of long-term financial planning. Upon receiving monetary gifts for his graduation, Marcus decided to open a Roth IRA. He researched different investment options and chose a low-cost index fund for his contributions. Understanding the power of compound interest, Marcus commits to contributing a portion of his earnings from his summer job before college. By starting to save for retirement at such a young age, Marcus is setting himself up for significant long-term financial benefits, showcasing the importance of early investment and retirement planning.

Sophia, a 16-year-old tech enthusiast, demonstrates how teens can use technology to manage their finances effectively. She uses a budgeting app to track her spending, categorizing each purchase and setting monthly limits for different expense categories. Sophia also set up automatic transfers from her checking account to a high-yield online savings account for her college fund. By embracing financial technology, Sophia has gained a clear picture of her spending habits and has been able to identify areas where she can cut back, such as reducing her spending on streaming services and putting that money towards her savings goals instead. Jake, a 17-year-old athlete, shows how teens can balance immediate wants with long-term financial goals. As a talented basketball player, Jake needs expensive equipment and training to improve his skills. However, he's also saving for college. To manage this, Jake created a prioritized spending plan. He saves money by buying some equipment second-hand and negotiates group discounts for training sessions with his teammates. Jake also referees junior basketball games on weekends, earning extra money that he splits between his equipment fund and college savings. His approach demonstrates how teens can find creative solutions to fund their passions while still saving for the future. Mia, a 15-year-old fashion lover, provides an example of how teens can indulge their interests while being financially responsible. Instead of buying new clothes regularly, Mia learned to sew and started upcycling thrift store finds. She turns her creations into content for her fashion blog and social media accounts, slowly building a following. Mia has even started selling some of her upcycled pieces online, turning her hobby into a small income stream. By finding a way to pursue her passion for fashion without overspending, Mia is learning valuable lessons about creativity, resourcefulness, and entrepreneurship.

David, a 16-year-old computer programming enthusiast, showcases how teens can invest in their skills for future financial benefit. Instead of spending money on video games, David uses his allowance and earnings from mowing lawns to pay for online programming courses. He's learning in-demand skills that he hopes will lead to internships and eventually a well-paying career. David's forward-thinking approach demonstrates how teens can make financial decisions that invest in their human capital, potentially leading to greater earning power in the future. Olivia, a 17-year-old animal lover, illustrates how teens can align their part-time work with their interests and values. She works part-time at a local animal shelter, earning minimum wage. While she could potentially earn more elsewhere, Olivia chooses this job because it aligns with her passion and provides valuable experience for her goal of becoming a veterinarian. To supplement her income, Olivia also offers pet-sitting services in her neighborhood. By choosing work that she finds meaningful, Olivia shows how teens can balance financial needs with personal fulfillment.

Tyler, an 18-year-old car enthusiast, provides an example of how teens can plan and save for big purchases. Tyler wants to buy a used car but is determined to do so without taking on debt. He created a dedicated savings account for his "car fund" and contributes a fixed percentage of his earnings from his part-time job at an auto parts store. Tyler also researches car prices, insurance costs, and maintenance expenses to understand the true cost of car ownership. His methodical approach to saving and researching demonstrates how teens can work towards significant financial goals responsibly. Zoe, a 16-year-old aspiring chef, shows how teens can turn their hobbies into learning opportunities and potential income streams. Zoe started a cooking blog where she shares budget-friendly recipes for teens and college students. She carefully calculates the cost per serving for each recipe, helping her readers understand food budgeting. Zoe uses the money she earns from ads on her blog to buy cooking equipment and ingredients for recipe testing. Her approach combines financial literacy, creativity, and entrepreneurship, showcasing how teens can explore their interests while developing valuable skills. Ryan, a 15-year-old gamer, demonstrates how teens can be savvy consumers in their areas of interest. Instead of buying every new game release, Ryan waits for sales, trades games with friends, and researches extensively before making purchases. He also earns store credit by trading in games he's finished. Ryan's approach to managing his gaming hobby shows how teens can enjoy their interests while being financially prudent, making informed decisions about their discretionary spending.

Jasmine, a 17-year-old honor student, provides an example of how teens can leverage academic success for financial benefit. Jasmine actively researches and applies for scholarships, treating the scholarship application process like a part-time job. She dedicates several hours each week to searching for opportunities, writing essays, and preparing applications. Jasmine's proactive approach to funding her education demonstrates how teens can take initiative in managing their future financial obligations. Lucas, a 16-year-old environmentalist, shows how teens can make financial decisions that align with their values. Lucas opened a checking account with a local credit union that invests in community development and green initiatives. He also researches companies before making purchases, choosing to support businesses with strong environmental and ethical practices when possible. Lucas's approach demonstrates how teens can use their financial choices to support causes they believe in, even with limited funds. Ava, an 18-year-old recent high school graduate, exemplifies how teens can prepare for the financial challenges of college. Before starting college, Ava took a free online course on personal finance to better understand concepts like student loans, budgeting, and managing credit. She also worked with her parents to create a realistic college budget, considering all potential expenses. Ava's proactive approach to financial education and planning showcases how teens can prepare themselves for the increased financial responsibilities of young adulthood.

These real-life examples demonstrate the diverse ways in which teenagers can effectively manage their money. From budgeting and saving to entrepreneurship and investing, these teens show that it's possible to develop strong financial habits at a young age. They highlight several key principles of good financial management:

1. Setting clear financial goals and creating plans to achieve them.

2. Distinguishing between needs and wants, and prioritizing spending accordingly.

3. Finding creative ways to earn money and develop valuable skills.

4. Using technology to track spending and automate savings.

5. Investing in personal development and future earning potential.

6. Aligning financial decisions with personal values and interests.

7. Planning for large purchases and long-term financial needs.

8. Being savvy consumers and researching before making significant purchases.

9. Taking initiative in financial education and preparation for future financial responsibilities.

10. Balancing current enjoyment with future financial security.

These examples also illustrate that effective money management for teens doesn't necessarily require large sums of money. Many of these teens are working with limited funds from part-time jobs, allowances, or small entrepreneurial ventures. What sets them apart is their thoughtful, intentional approach to managing whatever money they have. Moreover, these stories highlight the importance of financial education and literacy for teenagers. Many of these teens sought out information about personal finance, whether through online resources, books, or conversations with knowledgeable adults. This underscores the value of making financial education more readily available and accessible to young people.

It's important to note that while these examples are inspiring, every teenager's financial situation is unique. Factors such as family financial circumstances, access to earning opportunities, and personal responsibilities can all impact a teen's ability to manage money. However, the principles demonstrated in these examples – such as living below one's means, saving consistently, and investing in oneself – can be applied in various ways regardless of individual circumstances. In conclusion, these real-life examples of teens managing their money effectively provide valuable insights and inspiration for other young people beginning their financial journeys. They demonstrate that with the right knowledge, tools, and mindset, teenagers can lay a strong foundation for lifelong financial health and success. By starting early, these teens are not just managing their current finances effectively, but are also developing habits and skills that will serve them well throughout their adult lives.

Tracking your current spending and income is a fundamental step in managing your personal finances effectively. Here are some simple exercises that can help you gain a clear picture of your financial situation. These exercises are designed to be straightforward and accessible, particularly for teens or those new to personal finance management.

Interactive Financial Literacy Worksheet

1. The 30-Day Spending Log

What are your top three spending categories?

_____

_____

_____

What surprised you most about your spending habits?

_____

2. The Income Inventory

List your sources of income:

_____

_____

_____

What is your total monthly income?

$_____

3. The Cash Flow Calendar

On which dates do you typically receive income?

_____

On which dates do you have regular expenses?

_____

4. The Receipt Collection

What was your total spending this week?

$_____

Which category did you spend the most on?

_____

5. The Bank Statement Review

What percentage of your income are you spending on:

- Food: _____%

- Entertainment: _____%

- Transportation: _____%

- Savings: _____%

6. The Fixed vs. Variable Expense Sort

List your top three fixed expenses:

_____

_____

_____

List your top three variable expenses:

_____

_____

_____

7. The Savings Rate Calculation

What is your current savings rate? _____%

What savings rate would you like to achieve? _____%

8. The Cash-Only Week

How long did your weekly cash allowance last?

_____

How did using only cash change your spending habits?

_____

9. The Expense Ranking

What are your top three most important expense categories?

_____

_____

_____

Do these align with where you're currently spending the most? Yes / No

10. The Financial Goal Setting Exercise

What are your top three financial goals?

_____

_____

_____

How much do you need to save for each goal?

1. $_____

2. $_____

3. $_____

By when do you want to achieve these goals?

_____

_____

_____

These exercises are designed to be simple starting points for tracking your spending and income. They can be done individually or in combination, depending on what works best for you. The key is consistency – the more regularly you track your finances, the more accurate picture you'll have of your financial situation. Remember, the goal of these exercises isn't to judge your spending habits, but to understand them. Once you have a clear picture of where your money is coming from and where it's going, you'll be in a much better position to make informed decisions about your finances. As you become more comfortable with these basic exercises, you might want to explore more advanced tracking methods or budgeting apps. However, starting with these simple, hands-on exercises can provide a solid foundation for developing good financial habits and understanding your personal financial situation.

Chapter 2

BUDGETING 101: HOW TO CREATE AND STICK TO A BUDGET

A budget is a financial plan that outlines your expected income and expenses over a specific period, typically a month or a year. It serves as a roadmap for managing your money, helping you allocate your resources effectively and achieve your financial goals. At its core, a budget is a simple tool that allows you to track where your money comes from and where it goes, providing a clear picture of your financial situation and enabling you to make informed decisions about your spending and saving habits. Creating and following a budget is one of the most fundamental aspects of personal finance management. It's a practical way to take control of your financial life, regardless of your age, income level, or financial goals. For teenagers and young adults just starting to manage their own money, developing budgeting skills early can set the foundation for a lifetime of financial success and stability. The importance of budgeting cannot be overstated. It's the cornerstone of sound financial management, offering numerous benefits that extend far beyond simply tracking your income and expenses.

One of the primary advantages of budgeting is that it helps you live within your means. By clearly outlining how much money you have coming in and planning how you'll spend it, you can avoid overspending and accumulating debt. This is particularly crucial for young people who may be managing their own money for the first time and might be tempted to spend impulsively. Budgeting also plays a vital role in helping you achieve your financial goals. Whether you're saving for a new smartphone, planning for college expenses, or dreaming of buying a car, a budget provides a structured way to work towards these objectives. By allocating a portion of your income towards savings and tracking your progress, you can turn your financial aspirations into reality. This goal-oriented approach to money management can be incredibly motivating, especially for young people who may be working towards their first significant financial milestones.

Another key benefit of budgeting is that it increases your financial awareness. When you start tracking your income and expenses, you often discover spending patterns you weren't previously aware of. You might realize you're spending more on dining out or entertainment than you thought, or that small, frequent purchases are adding up to a significant amount over time. This increased awareness can lead to more mindful spending habits and help you identify areas where you can potentially cut back and redirect funds towards more important priorities. Budgeting also helps in preparing for unexpected expenses. Life is full of surprises, and not all of them are pleasant or affordable. By including an emergency fund category in your budget, you can gradually build up a financial cushion to handle unforeseen circumstances like medical emergencies, car repairs, or sudden loss of income. This financial preparedness can significantly reduce stress and provide peace of mind, knowing that you have resources set aside to handle life's curveballs.

For young people in particular, budgeting can be an excellent tool for learning delayed gratification – a crucial skill for long-term financial success. By planning your spending and saving, you learn to prioritize your financial goals over immediate wants. This skill of being able to resist the temptation of an immediate reward in favor of a later, often larger reward, is associated with better financial outcomes, as well as success in other areas of life. Budgeting also provides a framework for making informed financial decisions. When you have a clear understanding of your financial situation, you're better equipped to evaluate spending choices. For instance, if you're considering a significant purchase, your budget can help you determine whether you can afford it, how it might impact your other financial goals, and whether it aligns with your overall financial priorities. This analytical approach to spending can help prevent impulsive purchases and buyer's remorse.

Moreover, budgeting is an essential skill for developing financial independence. As young people transition into adulthood, managing their own finances becomes increasingly important. A budget serves as a practical tool for taking responsibility for your financial life, helping you understand the real costs of living and making independent financial decisions. This can be particularly valuable as you prepare for major life transitions like going to college, moving out on your own, or starting your first full-time job. Budgeting also plays a crucial role in debt management and prevention. For many young people, their first experience with debt often comes in the form of student loans or credit cards. A well-planned budget can help you understand how much debt you can realistically handle, guide you in making timely payments, and prevent you from taking on more debt than you can manage. By allocating funds for debt repayment in your budget, you can systematically work towards becoming debt-free or maintaining a healthy debt level. Additionally, budgeting can be a powerful tool for identifying opportunities to increase your income. As you track your expenses and compare them to your income, you might realize that you need to earn more to meet your financial goals. This realization can motivate you to look for ways to increase your income, such as taking on additional hours at work, starting a side hustle, or developing new skills that can lead to better-paying job opportunities.

Budgeting also fosters a sense of financial confidence. When you have a clear plan for your money and you're actively working towards your financial goals, it can boost your self-esteem and give you a sense of control over your life. This confidence can extend beyond your finances, positively impacting other areas of your life as well. For those planning to pursue higher education, budgeting becomes even more critical. College expenses go far beyond just tuition and books. A comprehensive budget can help you plan for all aspects of college life, including housing, meals, transportation, and personal expenses. By developing strong budgeting skills before college, you'll be better prepared to manage the financial challenges of student life and potentially reduce the amount of student debt you need to take on. Budgeting is also an excellent way to start learning about investing. As you become more comfortable with managing your income and expenses, you can start allocating a portion of your budget towards investments. This might begin with simply setting aside money in a high-yield savings account, but over time, it could expand to include other investment vehicles. The discipline and financial awareness you develop through budgeting provide a strong foundation for understanding more complex financial concepts and making informed investment decisions.

It's important to note that budgeting isn't about restricting your spending or depriving yourself of enjoyment. Instead, it's about making conscious choices about how you use your money. A well-planned budget should include allocations for fun and entertainment. The goal is to find a balance between enjoying the present and preparing for the future. By including discretionary spending in your budget, you can enjoy life's pleasures without guilt, knowing that you're doing so in a way that aligns with your overall financial plan. Budgeting can also be a valuable tool for developing and maintaining healthy financial communication habits. If you're part of a family, discussing budgets can open up important conversations about money, values, and goals. For couples, creating and following a budget together can strengthen your relationship by ensuring you're on the same page financially and working towards common objectives.

In today's digital age, budgeting has become more accessible than ever. Numerous apps and online tools are available to help you create and maintain a budget, track your spending, and visualize your financial progress. These technological aids can make budgeting less time-consuming and more engaging, especially for tech-savvy young people. However, it's important to remember that the tool itself is less important than the act of budgeting. Whether you use a sophisticated app or a simple spreadsheet, the key is to consistently track your income and expenses and use that information to guide your financial decisions. Budgeting also serves as an excellent introduction to the broader world of personal finance. As you become more comfortable with budgeting, you'll likely find yourself becoming curious about other financial topics. This natural progression can lead to a broader understanding of personal finance concepts, from saving and investing to insurance and retirement planning. In this way, budgeting can be seen as a gateway to overall financial literacy. It's worth noting that budgeting is not a one-time activity, but an ongoing process.

Your budget should be flexible and adaptable, changing as your life circumstances and financial situation evolve. As you grow older, your income may increase, your expenses may change, and your financial goals may shift. Regularly reviewing and adjusting your budget ensures that it remains relevant and continues to serve your needs. In conclusion, a budget is much more than just a list of numbers or a restrictive financial diet. It's a powerful tool that provides clarity, direction, and control in your financial life. By helping you understand where your money comes from and where it goes, a budget empowers you to make informed decisions about your finances. It allows you to align your spending with your values and goals, prepare for the future, and build a solid foundation for long-term financial success. For young people in particular, developing strong budgeting habits early can set the stage for a lifetime of financial well-being. Whether you're saving for your first major purchase, preparing for college, or simply trying to make the most of your current income, a well-planned budget is an invaluable ally in your financial journey.

The "50/30/20" rule is a straightforward and effective budgeting guideline that can help individuals, especially young adults and teenagers, manage their money more efficiently. This rule, popularized by Senator Elizabeth Warren and her daughter Amelia Warren Tyagi in their book "All Your Worth: The Ultimate Lifetime Money Plan," provides a simple framework for allocating your income across three main categories: needs, wants, and savings or debt repayment. The beauty of this rule lies in its simplicity and flexibility, making it an excellent starting point for those new to budgeting or anyone looking to streamline their financial management.

At its core, the 50/30/20 rule suggests dividing your after-tax income into three distinct categories:

50% for Needs: This category includes essential expenses that you must pay to maintain a basic standard of living. These are typically fixed costs and necessities such as rent or mortgage payments, utilities, groceries, transportation costs, and minimum debt payments.

30% for Wants: This portion of your budget is allocated to discretionary spending or non-essential expenses. These are the things that enhance your lifestyle but aren't absolutely necessary. Examples include entertainment, dining out, hobbies, subscriptions, and other lifestyle choices.

20% for Savings and Debt Repayment: This category is dedicated to building your financial future. It includes saving for emergencies, investing for long-term goals like retirement, and making extra payments on debts to reduce them faster.

The 50/30/20 rule is particularly valuable for young people who are just starting to manage their own finances. It provides a clear and easy-to-remember framework for balancing current lifestyle needs and wants with future financial security. By following this guideline, young adults can develop healthy financial habits early on, setting themselves up for long-term financial success. One of the primary advantages of the 50/30/20 rule is its simplicity. Unlike complex budgeting systems that require tracking every penny across numerous categories, this rule offers a broad overview that's easy to implement and maintain. This simplicity makes it more likely that individuals will stick to their budget over the long term. For teenagers and young adults who may find detailed budgeting overwhelming or time-consuming, the 50/30/20 rule offers a manageable entry point into responsible financial management.

The rule also provides flexibility, which is crucial for adapting to changing life circumstances. As your income or expenses change, you can adjust the allocations within each category while maintaining the overall structure. This adaptability makes the 50/30/20 rule suitable for various life stages and financial situations, from a teenager with a part-time job to a young professional starting their career. Implementing the 50/30/20 rule starts with calculating your after-tax income. For most people, this is the amount that appears on their paycheck. If you're self-employed or have other sources of income, you'll need to estimate your tax liability and subtract it from your gross income. Once you have your after-tax income figure, you can begin allocating it according to the rule. The 50% allocated to needs ensures that essential expenses are covered first. This priority helps prevent situations where discretionary spending might interfere with paying for necessities. For young people, understanding what truly qualifies as a need versus a want is an important learning experience. It encourages critical thinking about expenses and helps develop a realistic understanding of living costs.

The 30% allocated to wants allows for enjoyment and lifestyle enhancement without overspending. This category is where many people, especially young adults, tend to overspend, so having a clear limit can be helpful. It's important to note that this 30% is not meant to be spent in its entirety every month. If there's money left over in this category, it can be redirected to savings or debt repayment.

The 20% allocated to savings and debt repayment is crucial for building long-term financial security. For young people, starting to save early can have a significant impact due to the power of compound interest. This category also includes debt repayment beyond minimum payments, which can help reduce high-interest debt more quickly. For those without debt, this entire 20% can go towards savings and investments.

One of the strengths of the 50/30/20 rule is that it encourages a balanced approach to money management. It acknowledges that while saving is important, it's also okay to spend money on things that bring joy and enhance quality of life. This balance can help prevent feelings of deprivation that often lead to budget abandonment or financial splurges. For teenagers and young adults, the rule can be an excellent tool for developing financial awareness. By categorizing expenses as needs or wants, they learn to distinguish between essential and discretionary spending. This awareness can lead to more thoughtful consumption habits and a better understanding of personal financial priorities. The rule also promotes financial goal-setting. The 20% savings category encourages young people to think about their future financial needs and aspirations. Whether it's saving for a car, planning for college expenses, or starting to build a retirement fund, this allocation helps make these goals a tangible part of the budgeting process. It's important to note that while the 50/30/20 rule is a helpful guideline, it may need to be adjusted based on individual circumstances. For instance, in high-cost-of-living areas, people might need to allocate more than 50% to needs. Similarly, those with high levels of debt might need to allocate more than 20% to debt repayment. The key is to use the rule as a starting point and adjust as necessary to fit personal financial situations.

For young people just starting their careers or still in school, adhering strictly to the 50/30/20 rule might be challenging. In these cases, it's okay to start with what's feasible and gradually work towards the ideal allocation. Even if the initial split is more like 70/20/10, having a structured approach to budgeting is still beneficial. The 50/30/20 rule can also be a useful tool for financial communication within families. Parents can use this framework to teach their teenagers about budgeting and financial responsibility. It provides a clear structure for discussions about allowances, part-time job earnings, and saving for future expenses like college or a first car.

One potential challenge in applying the 50/30/20 rule is accurately categorizing expenses. Some costs may fall into a gray area between needs and wants. For example, a basic cell phone plan might be considered a need in today's connected world, but an expensive smartphone with a high-end data plan could be categorized as a want. These decisions require thoughtful consideration and can lead to valuable discussions about priorities and lifestyle choices. The rule also encourages mindful spending in the "wants" category. With a clear 30% allocation for discretionary expenses, individuals are prompted to prioritize their non-essential spending. This can lead to more satisfaction with purchases and a reduction in impulse buying. For young people, this aspect of the rule can be particularly beneficial in developing responsible spending habits. In the savings and debt repayment category, the 50/30/20 rule provides a framework for balancing different financial goals. Young adults might split this 20% between building an emergency fund, saving for short-term goals, and starting to invest for the long term. Those with student loans or credit card debt might focus more on debt repayment initially, gradually shifting towards savings and investments as their debt decreases.

The rule can also serve as a reality check for lifestyle inflation. As young people start earning more money, there's often a temptation to increase spending proportionally. The 50/30/20 rule provides a structure to manage income increases responsibly, ensuring that a portion of any raise or bonus goes towards financial security rather than being entirely absorbed by an expanded lifestyle. For those interested in personal finance, the 50/30/20 rule can be a gateway to more advanced financial concepts. As individuals become comfortable with this basic framework, they may become curious about topics like investment strategies, retirement planning, or more detailed budgeting techniques. This natural progression can lead to increased financial literacy and more sophisticated money management skills over time. It's worth noting that the 50/30/20 rule is not just about restricting spending, but about making conscious choices. By providing clear allocations, it allows individuals to spend money on things they enjoy without guilt, as long as it fits within the overall financial plan. This can lead to a healthier relationship with money, reducing stress and anxiety often associated with financial management. The rule also encourages regular financial check-ins. To maintain the 50/30/20 balance, individuals need to periodically review their spending and adjust as necessary. This habit of regular financial review is valuable for long-term financial health, helping to catch and correct any budgeting issues before they become significant problems.

For young entrepreneurs or freelancers with variable income, the 50/30/20 rule can be adapted by applying the percentages to average monthly income. This approach helps manage the financial uncertainty that often comes with self-employment or gig economy work. In the digital age, numerous budgeting apps and tools can help implement the 50/30/20 rule. These technologies can automatically categorize expenses, track progress towards goals, and provide visual representations of spending patterns. For tech-savvy young adults, these tools can make budgeting more engaging and less time-consuming. It's important to remember that the 50/30/20 rule is a guideline, not a strict rule. Its primary value lies in providing a simple framework for thinking about money allocation. Even if the exact percentages aren't always achievable, the principle of balancing current needs and wants with future financial security remains valuable.

In conclusion, the 50/30/20 rule offers a straightforward and effective approach to managing money, particularly well-suited for young adults and teenagers. Its simplicity makes it easy to understand and implement, while its flexibility allows it to be adapted to various financial situations. By providing a clear structure for allocating income between needs, wants, and financial goals, this rule helps develop crucial money management skills. It encourages mindful spending, promotes saving and debt repayment, and fosters a balanced approach to personal finance. While not a one-size-fits-all solution, the 50/30/20 rule serves as an excellent starting point for those looking to take control of their finances and build a solid foundation for future financial success. As young people navigate the complexities of personal finance, this simple yet powerful guideline can provide the structure and direction needed to make informed financial decisions and work towards long-term financial well-being.

Tracking income and expenses is a fundamental skill in personal finance management, providing a clear picture of your financial health and helping you make informed decisions about your money. For teenagers and young adults just starting to manage their finances, developing this habit early can set the foundation for lifelong financial success. Here's a comprehensive guide on how to effectively track your income and expenses:

Start with a Simple System:

Begin with a method that feels manageable and sustainable for you. This could be as simple as a notebook where you jot down all your income and expenses, or a basic spreadsheet on your computer. The key is to choose a system you're likely to stick with consistently.

Record Every Transaction:

Make it a habit to record every financial transaction, no matter how small. This includes all sources of income (allowance, part-time job earnings, gifts) and all expenses (purchases, bills, subscriptions). Capturing even small expenses is crucial as these can add up significantly over time.

Use Categories:

Organize your expenses into categories to get a clearer picture of where your money is going. Common categories might include:

- Food (groceries, dining out)

- Transportation (gas, public transit fares)

- Entertainment (movies, games, streaming services)

- Personal care (haircuts, toiletries)

- Clothing

- Education (books, school supplies)

- Savings

You can adjust these categories to fit your specific spending patterns and financial goals.

Keep Receipts:

Save receipts for all your purchases. This not only helps with accurate tracking but also provides a record in case you need to return an item or verify a charge later.

Set Regular Review Times:

Dedicate time each week to update your tracking system. This might be every Sunday evening or whatever time works best for your schedule. Consistency is key to maintaining an accurate record.

Utilize Technology:

Consider using budgeting apps or online tools designed for expense tracking. Many of these can link to your bank account and automatically categorize transactions, making the process more efficient. Popular options include Mint, YNAB (You Need A Budget), and PocketGuard. However, make sure to research the security features of any app before connecting it to your financial accounts.

Track Cash Expenses:

Cash transactions can be easy to forget, so develop a system for recording these. You might keep a small notebook with you to jot down cash expenses immediately, or use the notes app on your phone.

Be Honest and Accurate:

The purpose of tracking is to get an accurate picture of your finances, so be honest with yourself about your spending. Avoid the temptation to omit or underreport expenses you feel guilty about.

Separate Needs from Wants:

As you track your expenses, start categorizing them as either needs (essential expenses) or wants (discretionary spending). This distinction will be valuable when you start budgeting and looking for areas to potentially cut back.

Monitor Your Income:

While expenses often get more attention, it's equally important to track all sources of income. This includes regular income like allowance or part-time job earnings, as well as irregular income like gifts or freelance work.

Use Visual Aids:

Create simple charts or graphs to visualize your income and expenses. This can help you quickly identify trends and patterns in your financial behavior.

Keep Track of Savings:

Don't forget to track the money you're saving or investing. This is part of your financial picture and can be motivating to see grow over time.

Review and Analyze:

At the end of each month, review your tracked data. Look for patterns, areas where you might be overspending, and how well you're meeting your financial goals. Use this analysis to make adjustments to your spending habits or savings strategies.

Be Consistent:

Consistency is key in tracking. Even if you miss a day or two, don't give up. Just update your records as soon as you can and keep going.

Start Simple, Then Expand:

If tracking everything seems overwhelming at first, start by focusing on one or two categories that make up a large portion of your spending (like food or entertainment). As you get comfortable with the process, gradually expand to track all your expenses.

Use Tracking to Set Goals:

Once you have a clear picture of your income and expenses, use this information to set realistic financial goals. Whether it's saving for a specific purchase or reducing spending in a particular category, your tracking data will be invaluable in setting and achieving these goals.

Learn from the Process:

Tracking your income and expenses is not just about recording numbers; it's a learning process. Pay attention to how your spending aligns with your values and goals, and use this insight to make more informed financial decisions.

By consistently tracking your income and expenses, you'll gain a powerful tool for managing your finances. This practice provides the foundation for creating effective budgets, setting achievable financial goals, and developing healthy money habits that will serve you well throughout your life. Remember, the goal is not to restrict your spending, but to understand it and ensure it aligns with your financial objectives and values. Creating a basic budget using online tools or apps has become increasingly popular and accessible, especially for teenagers and young adults who are comfortable with digital technology. These digital solutions offer a convenient and often engaging way to manage personal finances, making the budgeting process less daunting and more interactive. The first step in creating a basic budget using these tools is to choose the right app or online platform that suits your needs and preferences. There are numerous options available, ranging from simple, straightforward budgeting apps to more comprehensive personal finance management tools. Popular choices for budgeting apps include Mint, YNAB (You Need A Budget), PocketGuard, and Goodbudget. Each of these apps has its unique features and interface, so it's worth exploring a few to find the one that feels most intuitive and aligns best with your financial goals. Many of these apps offer free versions with basic features, which can be an excellent starting point for those new to budgeting. Some apps also provide educational resources and tips, which can be particularly helpful for young people who are just beginning to learn about personal finance management.

Once you've chosen an app or online tool, the next step is to set up your account. This typically involves creating a username and password, and may also require you to provide some basic personal information. Security is a crucial consideration when using financial apps, so it's important to choose a strong, unique password and enable any additional security features offered by the app, such as two-factor authentication. After setting up your account, most budgeting apps will prompt you to connect your financial accounts. This usually includes checking and savings accounts, credit cards, and any loans you might have. By linking these accounts, the app can automatically import and categorize your transactions, saving you the time and effort of manually entering each expense. However, if you're not comfortable linking your bank accounts, many apps also offer the option to manually input your financial information. With your accounts connected or your information manually entered, the next step is to input your income.

This includes all sources of money coming in, such as allowance, part-time job earnings, or any other regular or irregular income. Most apps allow you to specify whether income sources are recurring (like a regular paycheck) or one-time (like a gift or bonus). Accurately recording your income is crucial as it forms the foundation of your budget, determining how much money you have available to allocate to various expenses and savings goals. Once your income is recorded, it's time to start categorizing your expenses. Most budgeting apps come with preset expense categories such as housing, transportation, food, entertainment, and others. You can usually customize these categories or add new ones to better reflect your specific spending patterns. As you begin to use the app, it will start to learn your spending habits and may suggest categorizations for your transactions, which you can confirm or adjust as needed. A key feature of many budgeting apps is the ability to set spending limits for different categories. This is where you can implement budgeting strategies like the 50/30/20 rule, allocating certain percentages of your income to needs, wants, and savings or debt repayment. The app will typically allow you to set these limits and will track your spending in each category, alerting you when you're approaching or have exceeded your set limits.

One of the advantages of using a budgeting app is the ability to easily track your progress towards financial goals. Most apps allow you to set specific savings goals, such as building an emergency fund, saving for a major purchase, or putting aside money for college expenses. You can usually specify the target amount and date for each goal, and the app will calculate how much you need to save regularly to meet that goal. This visual representation of progress can be highly motivating, especially for young people who might be saving for their first significant financial objective. Many budgeting apps also offer features for analyzing your spending patterns. They might provide visual representations like pie charts or graphs that show where your money is going each month. This can be eye-opening, especially if you've never closely tracked your expenses before.

You might discover that you're spending more in certain areas than you realized, which can prompt you to make adjustments to your spending habits. Another useful feature of many budgeting apps is the ability to set up alerts and notifications. You can often configure the app to send you reminders about upcoming bill payments, alerts when you're nearing your spending limit in a particular category, or notifications about unusual account activity. These alerts can help you stay on top of your finances and avoid overspending or late payments. Some apps also offer tools for planning future expenses. This can be particularly helpful for managing irregular expenses like annual subscriptions, car maintenance, or holiday gifts. By factoring these occasional expenses into your budget, you can avoid being caught off guard when they come due.

As you use the app over time, you'll be able to see trends in your income and spending. Most apps provide reports or summaries that show how your financial habits have changed over weeks, months, or even years. This long-term perspective can be invaluable in understanding your financial patterns and making informed decisions about your money. One of the challenges in using budgeting apps can be ensuring that all your transactions are correctly categorized. While apps have become increasingly sophisticated in automatically categorizing expenses, they may sometimes miscategorize transactions. It's important to regularly review your transactions and adjust categories as needed to maintain an accurate picture of your spending.

Many budgeting apps also offer features for sharing financial information with others. For teenagers, this might mean giving parents limited access to view their budgeting progress. For young adults, it could involve sharing budget information with a partner. These sharing features can facilitate important conversations about money and financial responsibility.

A unique aspect of using digital tools for budgeting is the gamification element that some apps incorporate. They might offer challenges, badges, or points systems that make the process of budgeting and saving more engaging and fun. This can be particularly appealing to younger users and can help maintain motivation to stick with budgeting over the long term. It's important to remember that while budgeting apps can make the process easier and more engaging, they are tools to assist you, not to make decisions for you. The app can provide information and suggestions, but ultimately, you are responsible for making financial decisions and sticking to your budget. Developing the discipline to follow your budget consistently is a crucial skill that goes beyond just using the app. As you become more comfortable with using a budgeting app, you might find yourself exploring more advanced features. Many apps offer investment tracking, credit score monitoring, or even basic financial advice. While these features can be useful, it's important to approach them with a critical eye and not rely solely on the app for complex financial decisions. One potential drawback of relying on budgeting apps is the risk of becoming overly dependent on technology for managing your finances. It's a good idea to maintain some basic financial management skills independent of the app, such as being able to calculate percentages or understanding how to balance a checkbook manually. These fundamental skills can serve as a backup and help you better understand the calculations the app is performing.

Privacy and data security are important considerations when using budgeting apps. Before connecting your financial accounts or inputting sensitive information, research the app's security measures and privacy policy. Look for apps that use bank-level encryption and don't sell your personal data to third parties. It's also worth noting that while many budgeting apps offer free versions, some of the more advanced features may require a paid subscription. Consider whether the additional features justify the cost, especially if you're on a tight budget.

Often, the free versions provide sufficient functionality for basic budgeting needs. As you use a budgeting app, you may find that your financial needs and goals evolve over time. Most apps allow you to adjust your budget categories, spending limits, and savings goals as needed. Regular review and adjustment of your budget is an important habit to develop, ensuring that your budget remains relevant and useful as your financial situation changes. In conclusion, creating a basic budget using online tools or apps can be an excellent way for teenagers and young adults to start managing their finances effectively. These digital solutions offer convenience, real-time tracking, and often engaging interfaces that can make budgeting feel less like a chore and more like a manageable part of daily life. By choosing the right app, setting up your accounts, categorizing your expenses, setting financial goals, and regularly reviewing your progress, you can gain valuable insights into your spending habits and take control of your financial future. Remember, the app is a tool to assist you in making informed financial decisions – the real power lies in the habits and discipline you develop in managing your money wisely. Meet Sarah, a 16-year-old high school junior with big dreams of attending college out of state. Growing up in a middle-class family in suburban Ohio, Sarah knew that paying for an expensive university would be a challenge. But she was determined to make it work. At the beginning of her sophomore year, Sarah sat down with her parents to create a budget and savings plan. They calculated that she would need to save at least $10,000 by graduation to cover her first-year expenses beyond what financial aid and scholarships might provide. It seemed like an overwhelming goal at first, but Sarah was motivated to make it happen.

She started by getting a part-time job at a local ice cream shop, working 15 hours a week after school and on weekends. Sarah committed to saving 75% of each paycheck, allowing herself to spend only a small portion on occasional movies or outings with friends. She meticulously tracked every dollar earned and spent in a budgeting app on her phone. Some months were harder than others - she had to resist the temptation to buy new clothes or go to expensive concerts that her friends were attending. But Sarah kept her eyes on the prize, visualizing herself walking across campus at her dream school. To boost her savings even further, Sarah looked for creative ways to earn extra money. She started a dog-walking and pet-sitting service in her neighborhood, marketing herself through local community boards and social media. During school breaks and summer vacation, she picked up additional shifts at the ice cream shop and babysat for families in need of childcare. Every time Sarah received cash gifts for birthdays or holidays, she put the money directly into her college fund instead of spending it. By the time Sarah started her senior year, her dedication had paid off. She had managed to save over $12,000 - exceeding her original goal. This financial cushion, combined with scholarships and financial aid, made it possible for Sarah to attend her top-choice university out of state. She felt an immense sense of pride knowing that her budgeting skills and work ethic had turned her college dreams into reality.

Jake's story is another inspiring example of a teen using budgeting to achieve an ambitious goal. As a 15-year-old freshman, Jake developed a passion for photography after taking an elective class at school. He dreamed of owning a professional-grade camera and lens kit, but the $3,000 price tag seemed impossibly out of reach. Jake's parents encouraged his interest but made it clear that such an expensive purchase would have to be entirely his responsibility. Undeterred, Jake created a detailed budget to map out how he could save for his dream camera over the course of 18 months. He started by cutting his discretionary spending to the bare minimum, forgoing video games, new clothes, and meals out with friends. Jake took on a paper route, waking up at 5 am every morning to deliver newspapers before school. He also offered to do yard work and odd jobs for neighbors on weekends. To keep himself motivated, Jake created a vision board with photos of the exact camera model. He wanted images representing the types of photography he hoped to pursue. He hung it prominently in his bedroom as a daily reminder of his goal. Jake tracked his progress meticulously, celebrating each time he hit a savings milestone.

There were moments of frustration along the way. Jake's friends didn't always understand why he couldn't join them for pizza after school or why he was working so much. He had to explain his goal repeatedly and stay focused on the long-term payoff. Jake also had to resist the urge to buy cheaper, lower-quality camera equipment that would have provided instant gratification but ultimately set him back from his real goal. After 16 months of disciplined saving and hard work, Jake finally reached his target. The day he walked into the camera store and purchased his dream kit with his own money was one of the proudest moments of his young life. Jake's budgeting skills not only allowed him to acquire the tools he needed to pursue his passion but also taught him valuable lessons about delayed gratification and financial planning that would serve him well into adulthood.

Mia's budgeting journey began when she was just 13 years old. Unlike many of her peers who received regular allowances, Mia's family struggled financially, and extra money was hard to come by. But Mia had always been a creative problem-solver, and she was determined to find a way to save for the things she wanted. It started with a desire to redecorate her bedroom. Mia envisioned a cozy, bohemian-inspired space that reflected her personality, but she knew new furniture and decor were out of the question given her family's tight budget. Instead of giving up on her dream, Mia decided to get creative with her resources. First, she made a detailed list of everything she wanted for her room makeover, from new curtains to wall art to bedding. Then, she researched affordable alternatives and DIY options for each item. Mia created a strict budget, allocating every dollar she could scrape together from babysitting gigs and selling old toys and clothes online. To stretch her limited funds, Mia became an expert at upcycling and repurposing. She scoured thrift stores and yard sales for secondhand treasures that she could transform with a coat of paint or new hardware. She learned to sew by watching online tutorials, allowing her to make her own pillowcases and curtains from discounted fabric. Mia's budgeting skills extended beyond just saving money - she also had to budget her time carefully to balance her DIY projects with schoolwork and other responsibilities. She created a schedule that allowed her to work on her room makeover for a few hours each weekend, slowly but steadily bringing her vision to life. Over the course of six months, Mia's dedication and resourcefulness paid off. She successfully transformed her bedroom into a personalized oasis, spending less than $200 in total. The experience taught Mia invaluable lessons about budgeting, creativity, and the satisfaction of working towards a goal. Her friends were amazed at the transformation and began asking Mia for advice on how they could makeover their own spaces on a budget.

Inspired by her success, Mia started a blog documenting her budget-friendly DIY projects and offering tips to other teens looking to decorate on a dime. Her ability to make the most of limited resources not only allowed her to achieve her immediate goal but also opened up new opportunities and sparked an entrepreneurial spirit that would continue to serve her well. For 17-year-old Alex, budgeting became a crucial skill when he decided to plan an epic road trip with friends to celebrate high school graduation. Alex and three of his closest buddies had always talked about driving across the country to visit national parks and major cities, but turning that dream into reality required careful financial planning. The group estimated that they would need about $2,000 each to cover gas, accommodations, food, and activities for their two-week journey. With nine months to go before their planned departure, Alex took the lead in creating a comprehensive budget and savings plan for the group. First, they broke down their expected expenses into categories: transportation, lodging, food, attractions, and emergency funds. Alex researched average costs for each category and built in a buffer for unexpected expenses. He then created a shared spreadsheet where each friend could track their individual savings progress and log any group expenses they covered. To reach their savings goals, each member of the group had to get creative. Alex picked up extra shifts at his part-time job as a grocery store cashier and started mowing lawns in his neighborhood. He cut back on unnecessary expenses like buying lunch at school and going to the movies, opting instead for packed lunches and movie nights at home with friends. One of Alex's friends, Maria, was particularly skilled at finding deals and discounts. She took charge of researching budget-friendly accommodations and free or low-cost activities in each city they planned to visit. Another friend, Jamal, used his coding skills to create a custom budgeting app for the group, making it easy for everyone to log expenses and track their progress in real-time. As the departure date approached, the group's excitement grew along with their savings accounts. There were a few close calls - like when one friend had an unexpected car repair that set back his savings - but the group rallied together to help him catch up. They organized a car wash fundraiser and picked up some shared gig economy jobs to boost their collective funds.

Thanks to Alex's meticulous budgeting and the group's dedication, they not only met but exceeded their savings goal. This allowed them to add a few extra experiences to their itinerary and gave them peace of mind knowing they had a solid emergency fund. The road trip itself was a transformative experience for Alex and his friends. They visited iconic landmarks, hiked breathtaking trails, and created memories that would last a lifetime. But beyond the sights and adventures, the process of budgeting and saving for the trip taught them all valuable lessons about financial responsibility, teamwork, and the rewards of careful planning. Lily's budgeting story revolves around her passion for music and her dream of attending a prestigious summer music program in New York City. As a talented violinist from a small town in rural Montana, Lily knew that this program could be a game-changer for her musical career. However, the program's tuition, travel costs, and living expenses in New York added up to a daunting $5,500. At 16, Lily was determined to make her dream a reality without placing a financial burden on her family. She started by creating a detailed budget outlining all the costs associated with the program and her stay in New York. Then, she devised a multi-pronged approach to reaching her savings goal over the course of 10 months. Lily's first step was to increase her income. She already gave violin lessons to beginners, but she decided to expand her student base and raise her hourly rate slightly. She created flyers advertising her services and distributed them around local schools and community centers. Lily also joined a local wedding music ensemble, which provided her with gig opportunities on weekends.

To supplement her music-related income, Lily took on a part-time job at a local bookstore. She committed to saving 90% of everything she earned, allowing herself only a small amount of spending money each month. Lily opened a separate savings account specifically for her summer program fund, making it easier to track her progress and resist the temptation to dip into the money. Lily also looked for creative ways to cut costs and earn extra money. She organized a series of benefit concerts in her community, with proceeds going towards her summer program fund. These events not only helped her financially but also gave her valuable performance experience and raised her profile in the local music scene. To save on everyday expenses, Lily became an expert at finding free and low-cost activities for hanging out with friends. She organized potluck dinners, movie nights at home, and hikes in nearby state parks. When she needed to buy something, Lily became adept at finding deals, using coupons, and shopping secondhand.

As her savings grew, Lily faced some challenges. There were moments when she felt. overwhelmed by her busy schedule and tempted to give up. The sacrifice of missing out on some social events with friends was particularly difficult. However, Lily remained focused on her goal, reminding herself of the incredible opportunity awaiting her in New York.

Lily's dedication paid off. Not only did she reach her savings goal for the summer program, but she also developed financial habits and skills that would benefit her for years to come. The experience of attending the music program in New York was everything Lily had hoped for and more. She returned home with improved musical skills, new connections in the industry, and a stronger sense of confidence in her abilities - both as a musician and as a savvy budgeter.

These stories of Sarah, Jake, Mia, Alex, and Lily demonstrate the power of budgeting and financial planning for teenagers. Each of them faced significant financial challenges in pursuing their dreams, whether it was attending college, buying expensive equipment, redecorating a bedroom, planning a epic trip, or participating in a career-changing program. Through careful budgeting, creative problem-solving, and unwavering dedication, these teens were able to turn their aspirations into reality.

Their experiences highlight several key lessons about budgeting: the importance of setting clear, specific goals; the value of tracking every dollar earned and spent; the need for discipline and sacrifice in the short term to achieve long-term objectives; and the power of thinking creatively about earning and saving money. These teens also learned the importance of staying motivated through visualization techniques, celebrating small milestones, and keeping their end goals in sight.

Moreover, the skills and habits these young people developed through their budgeting journeys - financial literacy, delayed gratification, resourcefulness, and perseverance - are invaluable life lessons that will serve them well into adulthood. Their stories serve as inspiring examples for other teenagers, proving that with proper planning, determination, and smart budgeting, even seemingly out-of-reach goals can be achieved.

Budgeting is a crucial skill for financial success, yet many people struggle to create and stick to an effective budget. One of the most common mistakes is failing to track all expenses. It's easy to remember big purchases or monthly bills, but small, everyday expenses can quickly add up and derail even the best-laid budget plans. Many people underestimate how much they spend on things like coffee, snacks, or impulse buys. To avoid this pitfall, it's essential to track every single expense, no matter how small. This can be done through various methods, such as keeping receipts, using a budgeting app, or maintaining a detailed spending journal. By capturing all expenses, you'll gain a true picture of where your money is going and identify areas where you can cut back if necessary.

Another frequent budgeting error is setting unrealistic goals. While ambition is admirable, setting overly aggressive savings targets or drastically slashing spending in multiple categories simultaneously can lead to frustration and ultimate failure. It's important to remember that sustainable budgeting is about making gradual, manageable changes. Instead of trying to cut your dining out budget by 80% overnight, aim for a more reasonable reduction of 20-30% to start. As you adjust to these changes and see progress, you can gradually increase your goals. This approach allows you to build momentum and confidence in your budgeting abilities, making it more likely that you'll stick to your plan long-term.

Neglecting to build an emergency fund is a critical oversight in many budgets. Life is unpredictable, and unexpected expenses can arise at any time – from car repairs to medical bills or sudden job loss. Without an emergency fund, these unforeseen costs can quickly derail your budget and potentially lead to debt. Financial experts generally recommend having three to six months' worth of living expenses saved in an easily accessible account. When creating your budget, make building and maintaining this emergency fund a top priority. Start by allocating a small percentage of your income to this fund each month, even if it means making cuts in other areas. Having this financial cushion will not only provide peace of mind but also help you stay on track with your other budgeting goals when unexpected expenses arise.

Many people make the mistake of creating a budget but then failing to review and adjust it regularly. Your financial situation and goals are likely to change over time, and your budget should reflect these changes. Life events such as getting a raise, changing jobs, moving to a new city, or starting a family can all significantly impact your income and expenses. Set aside time each month to review your budget and assess how well you're sticking to it. Look for areas where you consistently overspend or underspend and adjust your allocations accordingly. Additionally, conduct a more comprehensive review of your budget every few months or whenever you experience a significant life change. This regular maintenance will help ensure that your budget remains relevant and effective in helping you achieve your financial goals.

A common budgeting mistake is forgetting to account for irregular expenses. While monthly bills like rent, utilities, and loan payments are easy to remember, many people overlook less frequent costs such as annual insurance premiums, property taxes, or seasonal expenses like holiday gifts or summer vacations. These irregular expenses can throw off your budget if not properly planned for. To avoid this, make a list of all your non-monthly expenses for the year and divide the total by 12. This gives you a monthly amount to set aside for these costs. Include this amount in your regular budget as a "sinking fund" or "irregular expense fund." By spreading these costs out over the year, you'll be prepared when they come due and avoid the stress of scrambling to cover large, infrequent expenses.

Failing to distinguish between needs and wants is another frequent budgeting error. While it's important to allocate some money for discretionary spending, many people struggle to differentiate between essential expenses and optional ones. This can lead to overspending in areas that aren't truly necessary, leaving less money for important financial goals or necessities. When creating your budget, critically evaluate each expense and honestly categorize it as a need or a want. Needs are things essential for survival and basic quality of life, such as housing, food, utilities, and basic clothing. Wants are everything else – entertainment, dining out, the latest gadgets, or brand-name clothing. While it's okay to budget for some wants, prioritize your needs and financial goals first. Being clear about this distinction will help you make more informed decisions about where to cut back if necessary.

Many individuals make the mistake of not aligning their budget with their long-term financial goals. A budget shouldn't just be about managing day-to-day expenses; it should also be a tool for achieving your broader financial objectives. Whether your goals include saving for retirement, paying off debt, buying a home, or starting a business, your budget should reflect these priorities. Take the time to clearly define your short-term and long-term financial goals, and ensure that your budget includes specific allocations towards these objectives. This might mean setting up automatic transfers to a retirement account, allocating extra funds to debt repayment, or creating a savings category for a down payment on a house. By linking your budget to your larger financial picture, you'll be more motivated to stick to it and will see more meaningful progress over time.

A critical budgeting mistake is failing to budget for savings and treating it as an afterthought. Many people create their budget by subtracting their expenses from their income and then saving whatever is left over. However, this approach often leads to minimal or no savings, as there's rarely much left after accounting for all expenses. Instead, adopt the "pay yourself first" principle. This means treating savings as a priority expense and allocating money to your savings goals before budgeting for discretionary spending. Start by deciding on a percentage of your income to save – even if it's just 5% to begin with – and include this as a line item in your budget. As you get more comfortable with budgeting and find ways to reduce expenses, you can gradually increase this percentage. This approach ensures that saving becomes a habit and a non-negotiable part of your financial plan.

Overlooking the importance of budgeting for fun and personal enjoyment is another common error. While it's admirable to be disciplined with your finances, creating an overly restrictive budget that doesn't allow for any enjoyment can lead to burnout and ultimately cause you to abandon your budgeting efforts altogether. It's important to find a balance between responsible financial management and quality of life. Include a category in your budget for entertainment, hobbies, or other activities that bring you joy. This doesn't have to be a large amount, but having some funds allocated for fun can help you stay motivated and committed to your overall budget. Remember, the goal of budgeting is not to make yourself miserable, but to gain control over your finances and use your money in a way that aligns with your values and goals.

Many people make the mistake of not communicating about the budget with their partner or family members. In households where finances are shared, it's crucial that all adults are on the same page regarding financial goals, spending limits, and budgeting strategies. Lack of communication can lead to misunderstandings, overspending, and conflict. Schedule regular "money talks" with your partner or family to discuss your budget, review your progress, and address any concerns or necessary adjustments. If you have children, consider involving them in age-appropriate discussions about the family budget. This not only helps ensure everyone is working towards the same financial goals but also teaches valuable lessons about money management.

A significant budgeting error is relying too heavily on credit cards without a plan to pay them off. While credit cards can be useful tools for building credit and earning rewards, they can also make it easy to overspend and accumulate high-interest debt. Many people fall into the trap of using credit cards to cover shortfalls in their budget, telling themselves they'll pay it off later. However, this often leads to a cycle of debt that can be difficult to break. If you use credit cards, make sure to include the full payment in your monthly budget. Treat credit card spending as if it were coming directly out of your bank account. If you're carrying credit card debt, make debt repayment a priority in your budget, allocating as much as you can towards paying down the balance each month.

Another common mistake is not accounting for taxes correctly, especially for those who are self-employed or have multiple income sources. It's easy to look at your gross income and budget based on that number, forgetting about the chunk that will go to taxes. This can lead to a shortfall when tax time comes around. If you're an employee, make sure you understand your take-home pay after taxes and other deductions, and base your budget on this net amount. For self-employed individuals or those with significant non-wage income, set aside a percentage of your earnings for taxes in a separate account. Consult with a tax professional to estimate how much you should be setting aside based on your specific situation.

Many people make the error of not budgeting for professional development or skills enhancement. In today's rapidly changing job market, continuous learning and skill upgrading are crucial for career growth and job security. Failing to invest in yourself can limit your earning potential in the long run. Include a category in your budget for professional development expenses such as online courses, certifications, conferences, or relevant books. Think of this as an investment in your future earning capacity. Even if you can only allocate a small amount each month, consistently investing in your skills and knowledge can pay significant dividends over time.

A frequent budgeting mistake is failing to plan for major life transitions. Events such as getting married, having a child, buying a home, or retiring can have significant impacts on your financial situation. Many people fail to adjust their budgets in anticipation of these changes, leading to financial stress when the transition occurs. If you know a major life change is on the horizon, start planning for it well in advance. Research the potential costs associated with the transition and begin adjusting your budget accordingly. This might involve creating new savings categories, cutting back in certain areas, or finding ways to increase your income. By proactively planning for these transitions, you can make them smoother and less financially stressful.

Lastly, a critical budgeting error is giving up too quickly when things don't go as planned. Budgeting is a skill that takes time to master, and it's normal to have setbacks along the way. Many people abandon their budgeting efforts after a month or two if they overspend or fail to meet their savings goals. However, consistency and persistence are key to successful budgeting. If you find yourself consistently overspending in certain categories, take it as a learning opportunity. Analyze why it's happening and adjust your budget accordingly. Maybe your initial estimates were unrealistic, or perhaps you need to find creative ways to cut costs in that area. Remember that budgeting is a dynamic process, and it's okay to make adjustments as you go along. The important thing is to keep trying and learning from your experiences.

In conclusion, while these common budgeting mistakes can pose challenges, being aware of them is the first step towards avoiding them. Effective budgeting is about creating a realistic, flexible plan that aligns with your financial goals and lifestyle. It requires honesty, discipline, and regular review and adjustment. By steering clear of these common pitfalls and approaching your budget with patience and persistence, you can develop a powerful tool for achieving financial stability and working towards your long-term financial objectives. Remember, the goal of budgeting isn't perfection, but progress. Each step you take towards better financial management, no matter how small, is a step in the right direction.

Here's a step-by-step exercise to help you create your first budget.

Interactive Budgeting Worksheet

Step 1: Gather Your Financial Information

Check off the items you've collected:

☐ Recent pay stubs

☐ Bank statements from the last few months

☐ Credit card statements

☐ Bills (utilities, rent/mortgage, phone, internet, etc.)

☐ Receipts from recent purchases

Step 2: Calculate Your Monthly Income

List your income sources and amounts:

1. Salary/wages: $_____

2. Investment income: $_____

3. Rental income: $_____

4. Other income: $_____

   Total monthly income: $_____

Step 3: List Your Fixed Expenses

Write down your fixed expenses:

1. Rent/mortgage: $_____

2. Car payment: $_____

3. Insurance premiums: $_____

4. Student loan payment: $_____

5. Other loan payments: $_____

   Total fixed expenses: $_____

Step 4: List Your Variable Expenses

Estimate your monthly variable expenses:

1. Groceries: $_____

2. Utilities: $_____

3. Transportation: $_____

4. Phone and internet: $_____

5. Entertainment: $_____

6. Dining out: $_____

7. Shopping: $_____

   Total variable expenses: $_____

Step 5: Calculate Your Total Expenses

Total monthly expenses (fixed + variable): $_____

Step 6: Subtract Expenses from Income

Monthly income: $_____

Minus total expenses: $_____

Equals: $_____

Are you spending more or less than you earn?

_____

Step 7: Set Financial Goals

List your financial goals and monthly allocations:

1. Goal: _____ Amount: $_____

2. Goal: _____ Amount: $_____

3. Goal: _____ Amount: $_____

Step 8: Adjust Your Budget

Areas where you can cut back spending:

_____

_____

_____

Step 9: Choose a Budgeting Method

Which budgeting method will you use?

_____

Why did you choose this method?

_____

Step 10: Set Up a Tracking System

How will you track your spending?

_____

Step 11: Review and Adjust Regularly

How often will you review your budget?

_____

When is your next scheduled review?

_____

Plan to review your budget at least monthly. Compare your actual spending to your budgeted amounts and make adjustments as necessary. Remember, your first budget is a starting point - it will likely need refinement as you learn more about your spending habits and as your financial situation changes.

Remember, creating a budget is the first step towards greater financial control and achieving your money goals. Be patient with yourself as you learn this new skill, and don't be discouraged if you don't stick to your budget perfectly right away. With practice and persistence, budgeting will become easier and more natural.

Chapter 3

SAVING SMARTER, NOT HARDER

Saving money is a cornerstone of financial stability and long-term success. It provides a safety net for unexpected expenses, allows you to pursue life goals, and offers peace of mind in an uncertain world. The importance of saving cannot be overstated, as it empowers individuals to take control of their financial future and build a foundation for prosperity. Whether it's for emergencies, major purchases, retirement, or simply to have more financial freedom, cultivating a habit of saving is crucial for everyone, regardless of income level or life stage. One of the primary reasons saving is so important is its role in creating financial security. Life is unpredictable, and having savings can make the difference between weathering a financial storm and falling into debt. An emergency fund, typically recommended to cover 3-6 months of living expenses, can protect you from the financial impact of job loss, medical emergencies, or unexpected major repairs. This financial buffer not only provides practical support but also reduces stress and anxiety about potential future hardships. Saving also enables you to achieve both short-term and long-term goals without relying on credit or going into debt.

Whether you're saving for a down payment on a house, planning a dream vacation, or preparing for your child's education, having dedicated savings allows you to turn these aspirations into reality. Moreover, saving for specific goals can be motivating, giving you a clear purpose for setting aside money and helping you resist the temptation of unnecessary spending. One of the most compelling reasons to save is the power of compound interest. When you save and invest money over time, you don't just earn interest on your initial deposit – you also earn interest on the interest itself. This compounding effect can lead to significant growth over the long term, particularly when saving for retirement. The earlier you start saving, the more time your money has to grow, potentially leading to a much larger nest egg by the time you retire. To save effectively, it's essential to make it a priority and develop a systematic approach. Start by creating a budget that includes savings as a non-negotiable expense. Many financial experts recommend the "pay yourself first" method, where you allocate a portion of your income to savings before budgeting for other expenses. This approach ensures that saving becomes a habit rather than an afterthought.

Automating your savings is another powerful strategy for effective saving. Set up automatic transfers from your checking account to a savings account each payday. This removes the temptation to spend the money elsewhere and makes saving effortless. Many employers also offer direct deposit options that allow you to split your paycheck between different accounts, making it easy to funnel a portion directly into savings.

When it comes to where to keep your savings, it's important to choose the right type of account for your goals. For emergency funds and short-term savings, a high-yield savings account offers easy access to your money while typically providing better interest rates than traditional savings accounts. For longer-term goals, consider options like certificates of deposit (CDs) for slightly higher returns, or investment accounts for potential greater growth over time.

Diversifying your savings strategy can also lead to more effective saving. While it's important to have liquid savings for emergencies and short-term goals, don't overlook the potential for growth through investments. Depending on your risk tolerance and time horizon, consider allocating a portion of your savings to a diversified investment portfolio. This might include stocks, bonds, mutual funds, or index funds. Over the long term, these investments have the potential to outpace inflation and provide significant returns, though they do come with risks. Setting clear, specific savings goals can make your saving efforts more effective and motivating. Instead of a vague goal to "save more," define concrete targets like saving $5,000 for a vacation by next summer or accumulating $50,000 for a house down payment in five years. Break these larger goals down into monthly or weekly savings targets to make them more manageable and track your progress regularly. Another effective saving strategy is to look for ways to increase your income and immediately save the extra money. This might involve taking on a side hustle, selling items you no longer need, or negotiating a raise at work. By committing to save any windfalls or increases in income, you can accelerate your savings without feeling like you're sacrificing your current lifestyle.

It's also crucial to regularly review and adjust your saving strategy. As your income, expenses, and goals change over time, your saving plan should evolve as well. Conduct a savings check-up at least annually to ensure you're still on track to meet your goals and to identify any areas where you can increase your savings rate.

While saving money is important, it's equally important to balance saving with living a fulfilling life in the present. The goal of saving shouldn't be to deprive yourself of all enjoyment but to create a sustainable balance between current needs and future security. Allow room in your budget for experiences and purchases that bring you joy, while still prioritizing your long-term financial health.

Effective saving also involves being mindful of your spending habits and looking for ways to reduce unnecessary expenses. This doesn't mean living a life of extreme frugality, but rather being intentional about your purchases and ensuring they align with your values and goals. Often, small changes like cooking at home more often, canceling unused subscriptions, or finding free alternatives for entertainment can free up significant amounts of money for savings without drastically impacting your quality of life.

Remember that saving money is a skill that improves with practice. Don't be discouraged if you struggle at first or have setbacks along the way. The key is to stay committed to your savings goals and keep working at it. Over time, as you see your savings grow and experience the benefits of financial security, saving will likely become easier and more rewarding. In conclusion, the importance of saving cannot be overstated, and learning how to save effectively is a crucial life skill. By making saving a priority, automating the process, setting clear goals, and regularly reviewing your strategy, you can build a strong financial foundation that supports your current needs and future aspirations. Whether you're just starting your savings journey or looking to optimize your existing efforts, remember that every dollar saved is a step towards greater financial freedom and security.

With patience, discipline, and smart strategies, anyone can become an effective saver and pave the way for a more stable and prosperous financial future. When it comes to financial planning, understanding the difference between short-term and long-term savings is crucial for achieving a balanced and effective savings strategy. Short-term savings are typically earmarked for immediate or near-future expenses, usually within a timeframe of a few months to a couple of years. These funds are meant to cover anticipated costs or to serve as an emergency fund for unexpected expenses. Examples of short-term savings goals might include building an emergency fund, saving for a vacation, or setting aside money for holiday shopping. The primary characteristics of short-term savings are liquidity and safety, meaning the funds should be easily accessible and not subject to market fluctuations. As such, these savings are often best kept in high-yield savings accounts, money market accounts, or short-term certificates of deposit (CDs).

Long-term savings, on the other hand, are focused on future financial goals that are typically several years or even decades away. These savings are meant to fund major life milestones or to provide financial security in later years. Common long-term savings goals include saving for retirement, funding a child's college education, or saving for a down payment on a house. Because of the extended time horizon, long-term savings can often withstand more risk and volatility in pursuit of higher returns. As a result, these funds are frequently invested in a diversified portfolio of stocks, bonds, and other securities, often through vehicles like 401(k)s, IRAs, or brokerage accounts. The power of compound interest plays a significant role in long-term savings, allowing your money to potentially grow exponentially over time.

The approach to managing short-term and long-term savings differs significantly. Short-term savings require a more conservative approach, prioritizing capital preservation overgrowth. The goal is to ensure that the money is there when you need it, without risking loss due to market fluctuations. This often means accepting lower interest rates in exchange for security and liquidity. Long-term savings, however, can afford to take on more risk in pursuit of higher returns. The longer time horizon allows for riding out market volatility and potentially benefiting from overall market growth over time. This approach typically involves a more aggressive investment strategy, often with a higher allocation to stocks or other growth-oriented assets. Balancing short-term and long-term savings is key to a comprehensive financial plan. While it's important to have liquid funds available for immediate needs and emergencies, neglecting long-term savings can jeopardize your future financial security. Conversely, focusing solely on long-term goals while ignoring short-term needs can leave you vulnerable to debt or financial stress when unexpected expenses arise. A well-rounded savings strategy should address both time horizons, with the specific allocation depending on individual circumstances, life stage, and financial goals.

One effective approach to managing both short-term and long-term savings is to use a tiered savings strategy. This might involve keeping emergency funds and short-term savings in easily accessible accounts, medium-term goals in low to moderate-risk investments, and long-term savings in more growth-oriented portfolios. Regular review and rebalancing of this strategy is important, as your financial needs and goals are likely to evolve over time. As short-term goals are met or change, you may need to reallocate funds or adjust your savings priorities. It's also worth noting that the line between short-term and long-term savings can sometimes blur. For instance, saving for a home down payment might be a long-term goal for someone just starting their career, but a short-term goal for someone planning to buy in the next year. Similarly, an emergency fund is technically for short-term needs, but maintaining it is a long-term financial strategy. This fluidity underscores the importance of regularly reassessing your savings goals and adjusting your strategy accordingly.

Tax considerations can also play a role in how you allocate between short-term and long-term savings. Many long-term savings vehicles, such as 401(k)s and IRAs, offer tax advantages that can significantly boost your savings over time. However, these accounts often come with restrictions on withdrawals, making them unsuitable for short-term needs. Understanding these tax implications can help you optimize your savings strategy, potentially allowing you to save more efficiently for both short-term and long-term goals. Both short-term and long-term savings play vital roles in a comprehensive financial plan. Short-term savings provide the security and flexibility to handle immediate needs and unexpected expenses, while long-term savings lay the groundwork for future financial stability and the achievement of major life goals. By understanding the characteristics and purposes of each, and strategically balancing your savings between the two, you can create a robust financial foundation that serves your needs both now and in the future.

Remember, the key to successful saving is not just about how much you save, but also about saving smartly with a clear understanding of your goals and the most effective ways to achieve them. Creating a savings plan for emergencies and goals is a crucial step in achieving financial stability and working towards your aspirations. The first step in developing an effective savings plan is to clearly define your objectives. Start by establishing an emergency fund, which should ideally cover three to six months of living expenses. This fund serves as a financial buffer against unexpected events such as job loss, medical emergencies, or major repairs. Alongside your emergency fund, identify your personal financial goals, both short-term and long-term. These might include saving for a down payment on a house, planning a dream vacation, or building a retirement nest egg. Be specific about the amount you need to save and the timeframe for each goal, as this will help you create a more focused and motivating savings plan.

Once you've identified your emergency fund target and specific goals, the next step is to assess your current financial situation. Review your income, expenses, and existing savings to get a clear picture of where you stand. This analysis will help you determine how much you can realistically allocate towards savings each month. If you find that your current spending leaves little room for saving, look for areas where you can cut back. This might involve reducing discretionary expenses, negotiating better rates for services, or finding more cost-effective alternatives for your regular purchases. With a clear understanding of your goals and financial situation, you can now set specific savings targets. A common approach is to use the SMART criteria: make your savings goals Specific, Measurable, Achievable, Relevant, and Time-bound. For example, instead of a vague goal to "save more for emergencies," you might set a SMART goal to "save $6,000 for my emergency fund within 12 months by setting aside $500 per month." Break down your larger savings goals into smaller, monthly targets. This makes the process less overwhelming and allows you to track your progress more easily. Automating your savings is one of the most effective strategies for consistently meeting your savings goals. Set up automatic transfers from your checking account to your savings account(s) on payday or a specific date each month.

This "pay yourself first" approach ensures that saving becomes a priority rather than an afterthought. Many employers also offer the option to split your direct deposit between multiple accounts, allowing you to funnel a portion of your paycheck directly into savings before you have a chance to spend it. Automation removes the temptation to spend the money elsewhere and makes saving a habit rather than a conscious decision you have to make each month. Choosing the right savings vehicles for your emergency fund and various goals is another important aspect of your savings plan. For your emergency fund and short-term goals, consider high-yield savings accounts or money market accounts that offer better interest rates than traditional savings accounts while still providing easy access to your funds. For longer-term goals, you might explore options like certificates of deposit (CDs) for slightly higher returns, or investment accounts for potential greater growth over time. Remember to consider factors such as liquidity, risk tolerance, and time horizon when selecting the appropriate savings or investment vehicles for each of your goals.

Regularly reviewing and adjusting your savings plan is crucial for long-term success. Set up a schedule to review your progress monthly or quarterly. During these reviews, track your savings growth, assess whether you're meeting your targets, and identify any challenges or obstacles. If you find you're consistently falling short of your savings goals, revisit your budget to see if there are additional areas where you can cut back or look for ways to increase your income. On the other hand, if you're meeting your goals easily, consider increasing your savings rate or accelerating your timeline for reaching your objectives.

While building your emergency fund should be a top priority, it's important to balance this with progressing towards your other financial goals. Once you've established a solid emergency fund, you can start allocating more towards your other savings objectives. Consider using a percentage-based approach, where you divide your savings between different goals based on their priority and timeline. For example, you might allocate 50% of your savings to your emergency fund until it's fully funded, 30% towards short-term goals, and 20% towards long-term goals like retirement. Staying motivated throughout your savings journey can be challenging, especially when progress seems slow or when unexpected expenses arise. To maintain motivation, celebrate small victories along the way. Set milestones for each of your savings goals and reward yourself (in a budget-friendly way) when you reach them. Visualizing your progress can also be highly motivating – consider using a savings tracker or chart to visually represent your growth towards each goal. Additionally, remind yourself regularly of the reasons behind your savings goals and the peace of mind and opportunities they will provide once achieved.

It's also worth considering strategies to accelerate your savings. Look for ways to increase your income, such as taking on a side hustle, freelancing, or selling items you no longer need. Commit to saving any windfalls, such as tax refunds, work bonuses, or gifts, rather than treating them as extra spending money. You might also explore savings challenges or money-saving techniques to inject some fun and creativity into the process. For example, the 52-week savings challenge, where you save an increasing amount each week for a year, can be an engaging way to boost your savings.

Remember that creating and sticking to a savings plan is a skill that improves with practice. Don't be discouraged if you face setbacks or if progress is slower than you'd like. The key is to remain consistent and keep working towards your goals. As you see your savings grow and experience the security and opportunities they provide, you'll likely find that saving becomes easier and more rewarding. By developing a thoughtful savings plan and committing to it, you're taking a crucial step towards financial stability and empowering yourself to achieve your short-term and long-term financial aspirations. Compound interest is often referred to as the eighth wonder of the world, and for good reason. It's a powerful financial concept that can work either for you or against you, depending on whether you're saving and investing or borrowing money. At its core, compound interest is the process of earning interest on interest, creating a snowball effect that can lead to exponential growth of your money over time.

This concept is fundamental to understanding how wealth can be built through saving and investing, and why starting to save early can make such a significant difference in your long-term financial outcomes. To understand compound interest, it's helpful to first contrast it with simple interest. Simple interest is calculated only on the principal amount, while compound interest is calculated on the principal and on the interest accumulated over time. For example, if you invest $1,000 at 5% simple interest for 10 years, you would earn $50 in interest each year, totaling $500 in interest after 10 years. With compound interest, however, you earn interest not just on your initial $1,000, but also on the interest that accumulates each year. So in the first year, you'd earn $50, but in the second year, you'd earn interest on $1,050, and so on. This compounding effect leads to significantly more growth over time compared to simple interest.

The frequency of compounding can have a substantial impact on the growth of your money. Interest can compound daily, monthly, quarterly, or annually, among other frequencies. The more frequently interest compounds, the faster your money grows. For instance, $10,000 invested at 5% interest compounded annually would grow to $16,288.95 after 10 years. The same investment with interest compounded monthly would grow to $16,470.09. While the difference might seem small in this example, over longer periods and with larger sums, the impact of compounding frequency can be substantial. One of the most powerful aspects of compound interest is the effect of time. The longer your money has to grow, the more dramatic the effects of compounding become. This is why financial advisors often stress the importance of starting to save and invest as early as possible. Even small amounts invested early in life can grow to significant sums over decades. For example, if a 25-year-old invests $5,000 per year for 10 years and then stops, assuming an average annual return of 7%, by age 65, that $50,000 investment would have grown to over $600,000. In contrast, if someone starts investing the same amount at age 35 and continues for 30 years (investing a total of $150,000), they would end up with less money at age 65 – about $540,000. This illustrates the power of starting early, even if you can't continue investing for as long.

The Rule of 72 is a simple way to understand how compound interest can work in your favor. This rule provides a quick method to estimate how long it will take for your money to double at a given interest rate. Simply divide 72 by the annual rate of return to get the approximate number of years it will take for your investment to double. For instance, at a 6% annual return, it would take about 12 years for your money to double ($72 \div 6 = 12$). This rule helps illustrate how higher returns can dramatically accelerate wealth accumulation over time. While compound interest can work wonders for your savings and investments, it's crucial to understand that it can also work against you when you're in debt, particularly with credit cards. Credit card companies often compound interest daily, which can cause debt to spiral quickly if you're not paying off your balance in full each month. For example, if you have a $5,000 credit card balance at 18%

APR, and you only make minimum payments, it could take over 30 years to pay off the debt, and you'd end up paying more than $12,000 in interest alone. This demonstrates why it's so important to pay off high-interest debt as quickly as possible and avoid carrying balances on credit cards.

The power of compound interest becomes even more apparent when considering long-term financial goals like retirement saving. Let's say you start investing $500 per month at age 25, earning an average annual return of 7%. By the time you reach 65, your investment would have grown to over $1.2 million, despite only having contributed $240,000 of your own money. The rest – nearly $1 million – is the result of compound interest. If you waited until age 35 to start the same investment plan, you'd have about $566,000 at age 65. This ten-year delay could cost you more than half a million dollars in potential retirement savings, highlighting the importance of starting to save early. Compound interest can also play a significant role in building generational wealth. By starting to save and invest early, not only can you secure your own financial future, but you may also be able to leave a substantial legacy for your children or grandchildren. For instance, if you invested $10,000 in a diversified portfolio earning an average of 7% annually when your child is born, by the time they turn 65, that single investment could have grown to over $320,000, assuming you never added another penny.

This illustrates how relatively small financial decisions made early on can have profound impacts across generations. It's important to note that the power of compound interest is not limited to traditional savings accounts or investment portfolios. It can also apply to other areas of personal finance and wealth building. For example, reinvesting dividends from stocks or mutual funds allows you to purchase additional shares, which in turn generate more dividends, creating a compounding effect. Similarly, real estate investments can benefit from a form of compounding through appreciation and rental income reinvestment. Understanding compound interest can also help inform decisions about paying off debt versus investing. While it's generally advisable to pay off high-interest debt as quickly as possible, in some cases, the potential returns from investing might outweigh the interest savings from debt repayment. For instance, if you have a low-interest mortgage at 3%, and you have the opportunity to invest in a retirement account with potential returns of 7% or more, it might make more sense to invest extra funds rather than making additional mortgage payments. However, this decision should always be made carefully, considering factors like risk tolerance, tax implications, and overall financial goals.

The concept of compound interest also underscores the importance of being patient with your investments. In the short term, market fluctuations can be discouraging, but over long periods, the compounding effect tends to smooth out volatility. This is why many financial advisors recommend staying invested in diversified portfolios for the long term, rather than trying to time the market. The compounding effect works best when given time to operate, which means resisting the urge to withdraw funds or drastically change your investment strategy in response to short-term market movements. Another fascinating aspect of compound interest is its potential to create a "tipping point" in your wealth accumulation journey. In the early years of saving and investing, progress can seem slow, as the compounding effect hasn't had much time to work its magic. However, there often comes a point where the interest earned starts to exceed your regular contributions, and wealth accumulation accelerates rapidly. This tipping point can be incredibly motivating, as you see your money working harder for you than you are for it.

While the power of compound interest is undeniable, it's crucial to have realistic expectations about returns. Historical stock market returns have averaged around 10% annually before inflation, but it's prudent to use more conservative estimates when planning for the future. Additionally, returns are rarely consistent year over year – some years may see significant gains, while others may see losses. The compounding effect works over the long term to smooth out these fluctuations, which is why a long-term perspective is so important in investing. The concept of compound interest also highlights the importance of minimizing fees in your investments. Even small differences in fees can have a significant impact over time due to the compounding effect. For example, if you invest $100,000 over 30 years with a 7% annual return, the difference between a fund with a 0.5% expense ratio and one with a 1% ratio could be over $100,000 in total returns. This is why many financial advisors recommend low-cost index funds or ETFs for long-term investing. Understanding compound interest can also inform decisions about when to take Social Security benefits. While you can start receiving benefits at age 62, waiting until your full retirement age or even up to age 70 can significantly increase your monthly benefit amount. This increase is essentially a form of compound interest, as the additional amount you receive each month will add up substantially over your retirement years. The power of compound interest extends beyond just financial calculations – it can have a profound impact on your overall financial mindset and behavior. When you truly understand how compound interest works, you're more likely to prioritize saving and investing, resist unnecessary spending, and make financial decisions with a long-term perspective. This can lead to better financial habits overall, contributing to greater financial stability and security throughout your life.

It's worth noting that while compound interest can work wonders for building wealth, it's not a guarantee of financial success. It's still crucial to make wise investment decisions, diversify your portfolio, and adjust your strategy as your life circumstances and financial goals change. Additionally, factors like inflation can erode the purchasing power of your money over time, which is why it's important to aim for returns that outpace inflation in the long run.

In conclusion, the power of compound interest is a fundamental concept in personal finance that can have a transformative impact on your financial future. By starting to save and invest early, being patient, minimizing fees, and making informed decisions about debt and investments, you can harness the power of compound interest to build wealth over time. Whether you're just starting your financial journey or looking to optimize your existing strategy, understanding and leveraging compound interest can help you achieve your financial goals and secure a more prosperous future. Remember, time is one of the most valuable assets when it comes to compound interest – so the best time to start saving and investing is now. Saving for big purchases like a car or college education requires careful planning, discipline, and a strategic approach to managing your finances. The first step in this process is to clearly define your goal. Determine exactly what you're saving for, how much you need to save, and by when you need the funds. This clarity will help you create a focused and realistic savings plan. For example, if you're saving for a car, research the type of vehicle you want, its approximate cost, and factor in additional expenses like taxes, insurance, and maintenance. If you're saving for college, consider tuition fees, living expenses, books, and other associated costs. Having a specific target amount and timeline will make your goal more tangible and motivating.

Once you've established your savings goal, the next step is to assess your current financial situation. Review your income, expenses, and existing savings to determine how much you can realistically set aside each month towards your big purchase. This may involve creating or adjusting your budget to identify areas where you can cut back on spending and redirect those funds towards your savings goal. Look for non-essential expenses that you can reduce or eliminate, such as dining out, subscription services, or entertainment costs. Remember, every dollar saved brings you closer to your goal. Creating a dedicated savings account for your big purchase can be a highly effective strategy. This separation helps you track your progress more easily and reduces the temptation to dip into these funds for other purposes.

Many banks offer the option to set up multiple savings accounts or sub-accounts within your main account, often with the ability to name them according to your savings goals. Consider opening a high-yield savings account to earn more interest on your money as you save. While the interest rates on savings accounts are generally modest, every bit helps when you're working towards a significant financial goal. Automating your savings is a powerful tool for consistently making progress towards your big purchase. Set up automatic transfers from your checking account to your dedicated savings account on payday or a specific date each month. This "pay yourself first" approach ensures that saving becomes a priority rather than an afterthought. Start with an amount you're comfortable with, even if it's small, and gradually increase it over time as you adjust your spending habits or increase your income. Consistency is key when saving for big purchases, and automation helps remove the temptation to spend the money elsewhere.

For longer-term savings goals like college, consider exploring investment options that have the potential for higher returns than a traditional savings account. Depending on your risk tolerance and the time horizon for your goal, you might look into options like 529 college savings plans, which offer tax advantages for education savings, or a diversified investment portfolio of stocks and bonds. However, be mindful of the risks associated with investing and ensure that your strategy aligns with your timeline and risk comfort level. For shorter-term goals like saving for a car, it's generally safer to stick with more conservative savings vehicles to protect your principal.

Look for ways to accelerate your savings by increasing your income. This might involve taking on a part-time job, freelancing, or starting a side hustle. Dedicate all or a significant portion of this additional income directly to your savings goal. You might also consider selling items you no longer need or use and putting the proceeds towards your big purchase fund. Additionally, commit to saving any windfalls you receive, such as tax refunds, work bonuses, or monetary gifts, rather than treating them as extra spending money.

Track your progress regularly and celebrate milestones along the way. Saving for a big purchase can be a long-term endeavor, and it's important to stay motivated throughout the process. Set smaller, intermediate goals and reward yourself (in a budget-friendly way) when you reach them. Visual aids like savings trackers or charts can be helpful in maintaining motivation as you see your progress over time. Share your goals with friends or family members who can provide support and encouragement. Be prepared to make adjustments to your savings plan as needed. Life circumstances can change, and unexpected expenses may arise. Regularly review your progress and assess whether your current savings rate is sufficient to meet your goal within the desired timeframe. If you find you're falling behind, look for additional areas to cut back or ways to increase your savings rate.

On the other hand, if you're ahead of schedule, consider whether you can allocate even more towards your goal or if you want to set a more ambitious target. Consider breaking down your big purchase into smaller, more manageable goals. For instance, if you're saving for a car, you might set intermediate targets for the down payment, taxes, and insurance separately. This approach can make the overall goal feel less overwhelming and provide more frequent opportunities to celebrate your progress. For college savings, you might break it down by academic year or by specific expenses like tuition, housing, and books. Explore creative strategies to reduce the overall cost of your big purchase. For a car, this might mean considering a reliable used vehicle instead of a new one, or researching models known for their longevity and low maintenance costs. For college, look into scholarships, grants, and work-study programs that can reduce the amount you need to save. You might also consider starting at a community college for the first two years before transferring to a four-year institution to save on tuition costs. By reducing the total amount you need to save, you can make your goal more achievable or reach it faster.

Remember that saving for big purchases is a marathon, not a sprint. It requires patience, persistence, and sometimes sacrifice. However, the financial freedom and sense of accomplishment that comes from achieving your savings goal can be incredibly rewarding. By setting a clear target, creating a solid plan, automating your savings, and staying focused on your goal, you can successfully save for major purchases like a car or college education. This process not only helps you achieve your immediate financial objective but also builds valuable money management skills that will serve you well throughout your life.

Setting up a savings account is a fundamental step in managing your personal finances and working towards your financial goals. It provides a secure place to store your money while potentially earning interest, separating your savings from your everyday spending funds. The process of setting up a savings account might seem straightforward, but there are several important factors to consider to ensure you choose the right account for your needs and maximize the benefits of your savings efforts. Before diving into the specifics of how to set up a savings account, it's crucial to understand why having one is so important. A savings account offers a safe place to keep money for emergencies, future purchases, or long-term goals. It helps you resist the temptation to spend money that you've earmarked for savings, as it's typically separate from your checking account. Additionally, many savings accounts offer interest, allowing your money to grow over time, albeit usually at a modest rate.

The first step in setting up a savings account is to determine your savings goals. Are you saving for an emergency fund, a major purchase, or a long-term objective like retirement? Your goals will influence the type of savings account that's best for you. For example, if you're building an emergency fund, you'll want an account that offers easy access to your money. On the other hand, if you're saving for a long-term goal and don't need immediate access to the funds, you might consider accounts that offer higher interest rates in exchange for less liquidity, such as certificates of deposit (CDs) or high-yield savings accounts.

Once you've clarified your savings goals, it's time to research different types of savings accounts and the financial institutions that offer them. Traditional banks, online banks, credit unions, and financial technology companies all offer savings accounts, each with their own set of features, benefits, and potential drawbacks. Traditional brick-and-mortar banks often provide the convenience of in-person services and ATM access but may offer lower interest rates. Online banks, on the other hand, typically offer higher interest rates due to their lower overhead costs, but they may lack physical branches. Credit unions are member-owned institutions that often provide competitive rates and personalized service, but they may have eligibility requirements for membership.

When comparing savings accounts, pay close attention to the annual percentage yield (APY), which tells you how much interest you'll earn on your savings over a year. Look for accounts with high APYs to maximize your earnings. However, don't focus solely on the interest rate. Consider other factors such as minimum balance requirements, monthly maintenance fees, transaction limits, and ease of access to your funds. Some accounts may offer a high APY but require a large minimum balance or limit the number of withdrawals you can make each month. Ensure that the account's terms align with your savings goals and financial situation.

Another important factor to consider is the Federal Deposit Insurance Corporation (FDIC) insurance or, for credit unions, the National Credit Union Administration (NCUA) insurance. These government-backed insurance programs protect your deposits up to $250,000 per depositor, per institution, in case the bank or credit union fails. Always verify that the financial institution you're considering is FDIC or NCUA insured to ensure the safety of your savings.

Once you've chosen the type of savings account and the financial institution you want to work with, it's time to gather the necessary documentation to open the account. Typically, you'll need government-issued identification (such as a driver's license or passport), proof of address (like a utility bill or lease agreement), and your Social Security number. If you're opening a joint account, you'll need this information for all account holders. Some institutions may require additional documentation, so it's a good idea to check their specific requirements beforehand.

The process of actually opening the account will vary depending on the institution and whether you're opening the account online or in person. For online applications, you'll usually need to fill out a form with your personal information, agree to the account terms and conditions, and provide electronic signatures where necessary. If you're opening the account in person at a bank branch, you'll work with a bank representative who will guide you through the process and help you fill out the necessary paperwork. When opening your account, you'll typically need to make an initial deposit. The minimum amount required can vary widely between institutions and account types. Some accounts may have no minimum deposit requirement, while others might require several hundred or even thousands of dollars to open. Be prepared to transfer funds from an existing account or bring a check or cash if you're opening the account in person. After your account is opened, take some time to set up and familiarize yourself with the account features. Most banks offer online banking and mobile apps that allow you to check your balance, transfer funds, and manage your account settings. Set up online access to your account and download the mobile app if available. This will make it easier to monitor your savings and make deposits or transfers as needed. If your bank offers text or email alerts for account activity, consider setting these up to help you stay informed about your account status and any potential issues. One of the most effective ways to grow your savings is to set up automatic transfers from your checking account to your new savings account. This "pay yourself first" approach ensures that you're consistently saving before you have a chance to spend the money. You can typically set this up through your online banking platform or by speaking with a bank representative. Choose a transfer amount and frequency that aligns with your budget and savings goals. Even small, regular contributions can add up significantly over time thanks to the power of compound interest.

As you start using your new savings account, it's important to be aware of any fees or restrictions associated with the account. Many savings accounts limit the number of withdrawals or transfers you can make each month without incurring a fee. This is often due to federal regulations that historically limited certain types of withdrawals from savings accounts to six per month, although these regulations have been relaxed in recent times. Nevertheless, many banks still impose their own limits. Be sure to understand these restrictions to avoid unexpected fees. Regularly review your savings account to ensure it continues to meet your needs. As your financial situation changes or as you make progress towards your savings goals, you may find that a different type of account or financial institution better suits your needs. Don't be afraid to shop around and compare options periodically. The savings account market is competitive, and new products and better rates may become available over time.

Consider linking your savings account to other financial accounts to create a comprehensive financial management system. For example, you might link it to your checking account for easy transfers, or to investment accounts if you're saving for long-term goals. Some banks offer the ability to create sub-accounts or multiple savings accounts under one main account, which can be useful for organizing your savings for different goals.

As you build your savings, it's crucial to maintain good security practices to protect your money. Use strong, unique passwords for your online banking access and consider enabling two-factor authentication if available. Be cautious about sharing your account information and be wary of phishing attempts or suspicious emails claiming to be from your bank. Regularly monitor your account for any unauthorized transactions and report any suspicious activity to your bank immediately.

Remember that setting up a savings account is just the first step in your savings journey. To truly benefit from your account, you need to consistently contribute to it and resist the temptation to withdraw funds unnecessarily. Treat your savings as a non-negotiable expense in your budget, just like rent or utilities. Over time, as you see your balance grow, you'll likely feel more motivated to continue and even increase your savings efforts.

If you're having trouble consistently saving, consider using psychological tricks to make the process easier. For example, you might use the "52-week money challenge," where you save $1 the first week, $2 the second week, and so on, until you're saving $52 in the final week of the year. This gradual approach can make saving feel more manageable and even fun. Alternatively, you could use a "round-up" savings app that automatically rounds up your purchases to the nearest dollar and deposits the difference into your savings account. As your savings grow, you might consider diversifying your savings strategy. While a basic savings account is a great starting point, you may want to explore other options for different financial goals. For short to medium-term goals, you might look into money market accounts or certificates of deposit (CDs) that may offer higher interest rates. For long-term goals like retirement, you might consider investment accounts that have the potential for higher returns, albeit with more risk. Setting up and maintaining a savings account is a crucial step in taking control of your financial future. It provides a foundation for financial stability, helps you work towards your goals, and can give you peace of mind knowing you have funds set aside for emergencies or future opportunities. By choosing the right account, consistently contributing to it, and regularly reviewing your savings strategy, you can make significant progress towards your financial objectives. Remember, the journey to financial well-being is a marathon, not a sprint. Every dollar you save is a step in the right direction, and over time, these small steps can lead to significant financial security and freedom.

Setting realistic savings goals is a crucial step in achieving financial stability and working towards your aspirations. This exercise will guide you through the process of establishing attainable savings targets that align with your personal circumstances and objectives. Let's begin by breaking down the goal-setting process into manageable steps.

Interactive Savings Goals Worksheet

Step 1: Assess Your Current Financial Situation

Monthly net income: $_____

List your monthly expenses:

	: $
	: $
	: $
	: $
	: $

Total monthly expenses: $_____

Money available for saving (income minus expenses): $_____

Step 2: Identify Your Savings Priorities

List your savings goals:

_____

_____

_____

_____

_____

Step 3: Prioritize Your Goals

Rank your goals from most to least important:

_____

_____

_____

_____

_____

Step 4: Set Specific Targets for Each Goal

Goal 1: _____

Total amount: $_____

Timeframe: _____

Monthly savings required: $_____

Goal 2: _____

Total amount: $_____

Timeframe: _____

Monthly savings required: $_____

Goal 3: _____

Total amount: $_____

Timeframe: _____

Monthly savings required: $_____

Step 5: Evaluate the Feasibility of Your Goals

Can you realistically save these amounts each month?

_____

Do you need to adjust your spending to meet these savings goals?

_____

Are there any goals that might need a longer timeframe or reduced target amount?

_____

Step 6: Adjust Your Goals if Necessary

List any adjustments you need to make to your goals:

_____

_____

_____

Step 7: Create a Savings Plan

For each goal, which savings vehicle will you use?

Goal 1:

_____

Goal 2:

_____

Goal 3:

_____

How will you track your progress?

_____

Step 8: Review and Revise Regularly

How often will you review your progress?

_____

Date of your first progress review:

_____

Exercise:

1. Current monthly income: $_____

   Current monthly expenses: $_____

2. List three savings goals:

   _____

   _____

   _____

3. For each goal:

   Goal 1: Total amount: $_____ Timeframe: _____

   Goal 2: Total amount: $_____ Timeframe: _____

   Goal 3: Total amount: $_____ Timeframe: _____

4. Calculate monthly savings required:

   Goal 1: $_____

   Goal 2: $_____

   Goal 3: $_____

5. Are these monthly savings amounts feasible?

   _____

6. If necessary, list adjustments to make goals more realistic:

   _____

7. Specific actions to start working towards these goals:

   _____

   _____

   _____

8. Date for first progress review:

   _____

By completing this exercise, you'll have a clear, realistic savings plan tailored to your personal financial situation and goals. Remember, the key to successful saving is consistency and adaptability. Start small if needed, and gradually increase your savings as your financial situation improves. With patience and persistence, you'll be well on your way to achieving your financial aspirations.

Chapter 4

MASTERING
THE ART OF SMART SPENDING

Understanding the difference between needs and wants is a crucial aspect of personal finance and budgeting. At its core, this distinction helps individuals prioritize their spending, make informed financial decisions, and achieve a balance between necessary expenses and discretionary purchases. Needs are typically defined as items or services that are essential for survival and basic well-being, while wants are desires that enhance our life but are not strictly necessary for survival. However, the line between needs and wants can often be blurry, and what constitutes a need versus a want can vary depending on individual circumstances, cultural context, and personal values. Needs generally fall into several basic categories: food, water, shelter, clothing, healthcare, and in today's society, often basic transportation and communication. These are the essentials required to maintain health, safety, and the ability to work and function in society. For example, nutritious food is a need, but dining out at expensive restaurants is typically considered a want. Basic clothing to protect from the elements and maintain social norms is a need, but designer fashion or excessive quantities of clothing fall into the want category. Shelter is a need, but a large house with luxury amenities is a want. It's important to note that even within these need categories, there can be a spectrum from basic necessity to luxury.

Wants, on the other hand, encompass a wide range of goods and services that make life more enjoyable but are not essential for survival or basic functioning. This can include entertainment, travel, hobbies, luxury items, upgraded versions of basic goods, and many other purchases that bring pleasure or convenience but aren't strictly necessary. While wants are not essential, they play a significant role in our quality of life, personal fulfillment, and happiness. The key is finding a balance between addressing needs and allowing for wants within the constraints of one's financial situation. One of the challenges in distinguishing between needs and wants is that many items can fall into a gray area, depending on context. For instance, a car might be considered a want in a city with excellent public transportation, but it could be a need for someone living in a rural area with no other means of getting to work. Similarly, a smartphone might be seen as a want by some, but in today's digital age, it could be considered a need for many professionals who require constant connectivity for their work. Education is another area that blurs the line – while basic education is generally considered a need, higher education or specialized training might be seen as a want by some and a need by others, depending on career goals and personal circumstances. Cultural and societal norms also play a role in shaping our perceptions of needs and wants. What is considered a basic need in one society might be viewed as a luxury in another. For example, air conditioning might be seen as a want in temperate climates but could be considered a need in extremely hot regions. Similarly, cultural expectations around clothing, food, and social activities can influence whether certain purchases are perceived as needs or wants. It's important to be aware of these influences and critically evaluate whether societal pressures are driving us to categorize wants as needs.

Personal values and priorities also factor into the needs versus wants equation. For some, regular exercise might be considered a need for maintaining physical and mental health, which could justify expenses related to gym memberships or home exercise equipment. Others might view these as wants. Similarly, some individuals might consider investing in personal growth and education a need, while others might categorize it as a want. These personal interpretations highlight the subjective nature of the needs versus wants distinction and underscore the importance of aligning spending with individual values and goals. From a financial planning perspective, distinguishing between needs and wants is crucial for creating an effective budget and achieving financial stability. By clearly identifying needs, individuals can ensure that these essential expenses are covered first, before allocating funds to wants. This prioritization helps prevent situations where discretionary spending on wants leaves insufficient funds for critical needs. It also aids in building a robust emergency fund, as understanding true needs helps in calculating how much should be set aside for unexpected circumstances.

When it comes to budgeting, a common approach is the 50/30/20 rule, where 50% of income is allocated to needs, 30% to wants, and 20% to savings and debt repayment. While these percentages can be adjusted based on individual circumstances, this framework provides a starting point for balancing essential expenses with discretionary spending and financial goals. By categorizing expenses as needs or wants, individuals can more easily identify areas where they might be overspending on non-essentials and find opportunities to redirect funds towards savings or debt reduction. It's important to note that completely eliminating wants from one's budget is neither realistic nor desirable for most people. Wants contribute to our quality of life, provide motivation, and can be important for mental health and overall well-being. The goal is not to live a life devoid of pleasure or indulgence, but rather to find a sustainable balance that allows for enjoyment while ensuring financial stability and progress towards long-term goals. This balance might involve finding less expensive ways to fulfill wants, prioritizing certain wants over others, or finding free or low-cost alternatives that provide similar satisfaction.

One effective strategy for managing the balance between needs and wants is to implement a waiting period before making non-essential purchases. This can help distinguish between genuine wants and impulsive desires. For example, adopting a 24-hour or 7-day rule before buying non-essential items can provide time for reflection on whether the purchase aligns with personal values and financial goals. This waiting period often reveals that many wants are fleeting desires rather than items that will provide lasting satisfaction or value. Another approach to managing wants is to practice mindful spending. This involves being fully present and aware when making purchasing decisions, considering not just the immediate gratification but also the long-term impact of the purchase. Mindful spending encourages individuals to question their motivations for wanting certain items and to consider whether there might be non-material ways to fulfill the underlying desires or needs that drive these wants. It's also valuable to regularly reassess what constitutes a need versus a want in your life. As circumstances change, so too might the categorization of certain expenses. What was once a want might become a need due to changes in work, family situations, or health. Conversely, what was previously considered a need might become a want as lifestyles or priorities shift. This ongoing evaluation helps ensure that spending remains aligned with current life situations and goals.

When trying to reduce spending on wants, it can be helpful to focus on finding alternative ways to fulfill the underlying needs or desires. For example, if eating out is a want that's straining your budget, consider the underlying motivations – is it about the food itself, social connection, or a break from cooking? Once identified, you can explore less expensive alternatives that fulfill the same need, such as hosting potluck dinners with friends or learning to cook new, exciting meals at home. It's also important to recognize the role of marketing and social influences in shaping our perceptions of needs and wants. Advertising often aims to create a sense of need for products that are, in reality, wants. Social media and peer pressure can also contribute to a blurring of the lines between needs and wants, as we're constantly exposed to others' consumption habits and lifestyle choices. Developing a critical eye towards these influences and staying grounded in personal values can help maintain a clearer distinction between true needs and externally-influenced wants. For families, discussing and agreeing on what constitutes needs versus wants can be a valuable exercise. This not only helps in creating a unified approach to family finances but also provides an opportunity to teach children about financial priorities and decision-making. Involving children in discussions about household needs and wants can help them develop a healthy perspective on money and consumption from an early age.

In some cases, what starts as a want can evolve into a need over time. For instance, a car might initially be purchased as a want for convenience, but if life circumstances change (such as a job requiring extensive travel), it could become a need. This evolution underscores the importance of flexibility in financial planning and the need to periodically reassess and adjust budgets and spending priorities.

Ultimately, the distinction between needs and wants is a personal one that requires honest self-reflection and alignment with individual values and goals. While there are general guidelines, the specific categorization can vary greatly from person to person. The key is to develop a clear understanding of what truly constitutes a need in your life and to approach wants with mindfulness and intentionality. By cultivating a nuanced understanding of needs versus wants, individuals can make more informed financial decisions, create more effective budgets, and find a balance that allows for both financial stability and personal enjoyment. This understanding forms the foundation for sound financial management, helping to ensure that essential needs are met while still allowing room for the wants that contribute to a fulfilling life. Remember, the goal is not to eliminate all wants, but to prioritize spending in a way that aligns with personal values and financial objectives, leading to greater financial health and overall life satisfaction. Impulse buying can be a significant obstacle to achieving financial goals and maintaining a healthy budget. This unplanned, spur-of-the-moment type of purchasing is often driven by emotions rather than necessity, leading to regret and financial strain. To avoid falling into the trap of impulse buying, it's crucial to develop strategies that help you make more thoughtful, deliberate purchasing decisions. One of the most effective ways to curb impulse buying is to create a shopping list before heading to stores or browsing online. By sticking to this list, you're less likely to be swayed by attractive displays or enticing sales on items you don't truly need. This simple act of planning can significantly reduce the temptation to make unplanned purchases.

Another powerful strategy is to implement a waiting period before making non-essential purchases. This could be a 24-hour rule for smaller items or a 30-day rule for larger expenses. During this cooling-off period, you can evaluate whether the item is truly necessary or if the desire to buy was simply a fleeting impulse. Often, you'll find that the urge to purchase passes, and you're grateful you didn't give in to the momentary desire. This waiting period also allows you to research the item further, compare prices, and consider if there are better alternatives or if you already own something that serves the same purpose. Understanding your triggers for impulse buying is crucial in avoiding it. Common triggers include stress, boredom, social pressure, or the fear of missing out on a good deal. By identifying what prompts you to make impulsive purchases, you can develop strategies to address these triggers in healthier ways. For instance, if you tend to shop when stressed, you might explore stress-relief techniques like exercise or meditation instead of turning to retail therapy. If social media advertising frequently tempts you, consider limiting your exposure to these platforms or using ad-blocking tools.

Practicing mindful spending is another effective way to combat impulse buying. This involves being fully present and aware when making purchasing decisions. Before buying something, ask yourself questions like: "Do I really need this?", "How will this improve my life?", "Is this aligned with my financial goals and values?". By consciously evaluating each purchase, you're more likely to make decisions that truly benefit you in the long run, rather than succumbing to momentary desires. Avoiding situations that tempt you to impulse buy can also be helpful. This might mean unsubscribing from retailer email lists, avoiding window shopping or browsing online stores when you're bored, and steering clear of sales unless you have a specific, pre-planned purchase in mind. Remember, you can't be tempted by what you don't see, so limiting your exposure to marketing messages and shopping environments can significantly reduce impulse buying.

Setting clear financial goals and regularly reminding yourself of these objectives can provide motivation to resist impulse purchases. When you're tempted to buy something on impulse, take a moment to reflect on your larger financial aspirations, whether it's saving for a home, paying off debt, or building an emergency fund. Visualizing these goals and the progress you've made towards them can often provide the willpower needed to walk away from an unnecessary purchase.

Using cash instead of credit cards for discretionary spending can also help curb impulse buying. The physical act of handing over cash makes the spending feel more real and can cause you to think twice before making a purchase. Additionally, limiting yourself to a set amount of cash for non-essential spending creates a natural boundary that's harder to cross than the seemingly limitless nature of credit cards.

Educating yourself about marketing tactics and consumer psychology can make you more resistant to impulse buying. Understanding how retailers use tactics like limited-time offers, strategic pricing, and product placement to encourage impulse purchases can help you recognize and resist these influences. Knowledge is power, and being aware of these strategies can help you make more rational, less emotionally-driven purchasing decisions. Creating a budget and tracking your expenses is another crucial step in avoiding impulse buying. When you have a clear picture of your income and necessary expenses, and you've allocated specific amounts for different spending categories, you're more likely to think twice before making an unplanned purchase that could throw your budget off balance. Use budgeting apps or spreadsheets to keep track of your spending and regularly review your expenses to ensure you're sticking to your financial plan. Finally, finding non-material sources of happiness and fulfillment can reduce the urge to impulse buy. Often, impulse purchases are an attempt to fill an emotional need or provide a quick boost of happiness. By cultivating hobbies, relationships, and experiences that bring joy and satisfaction without requiring spending, you can reduce the emotional pull of impulse buying. Engage in activities like exercising, reading, spending time in nature, or connecting with friends and family – these can provide lasting happiness without the financial burden of unnecessary purchases.

Remember, avoiding impulse buying is a skill that improves with practice. Don't be discouraged if you occasionally slip up; instead, use it as a learning opportunity to understand what triggered the impulse and how you can better resist it in the future. With consistent effort and the application of these strategies, you can significantly reduce impulse buying, leading to better financial health and greater overall satisfaction with your purchasing decisions. Making smart decisions when spending money is crucial for building a solid financial foundation, especially for teenagers who are just starting to manage their own finances. Begin by understanding the difference between needs and wants. Needs are essentials such as food, clothing, and education, while wants are additional comforts or luxuries. Prioritize spending on needs first to ensure your basic requirements are met before indulging in non-essential items.

Next, create a budget to manage your money effectively. This involves tracking your income and expenses to see where your money goes and ensuring you don't spend more than you earn. Use this budget to set spending limits and stick to them. Consider adopting the 24-hour rule for discretionary purchases; if you see something you want, wait 24 hours before buying it. This pause can help you assess whether the purchase is truly necessary or if you're just experiencing a momentary impulse. Additionally, always look for ways to get the best value for your money. Compare prices before making a purchase and look for discounts or deals. Avoid high-interest debt, such as credit card debt, which can quickly become a financial burden. Instead, save up for items you want to buy or find alternatives that fit within your budget. Finally, consider the long-term impact of your spending decisions. Think about how your purchases will affect your financial goals, such as saving for a car, college, or future emergencies. By making thoughtful, informed spending decisions, you'll not only avoid unnecessary debt but also build healthy financial habits that will benefit you throughout your life. Finding discounts and deals is a valuable skill that can greatly enhance your purchasing power and stretch your budget.

One effective strategy is to utilize online resources, such as coupon websites like RetailMeNot, Coupons.com, and Honey, which compile promotional codes and offers from various retailers. These sites often feature a range of discounts, including percentage-off deals and free shipping offers. Signing up for email newsletters from your favorite stores can also be beneficial, as many retailers send exclusive offers and promotional codes to their subscribers, giving early access to sales and special deals. Additionally, mobile apps are powerful tools for finding discounts. Apps like Rakuten (formerly Ebates) provide cashback on purchases made through their platform, while others like Ibotta offer cashback on groceries and everyday items. Many store-specific apps offer app-only deals and loyalty rewards, and enabling notifications for these apps can help you stay informed about new promotions. Comparing prices before making a purchase is another important tactic. Websites such as Google Shopping and PriceGrabber allow you to search for products and view their prices at various online stores, helping you identify the best deals and avoid overpaying. It's also worthwhile to check local stores and their online counterparts, as price variations can be significant. Seasonal sales present additional opportunities for savings. Major holidays like Black Friday and Cyber Monday, as well as end-of-season sales, offer substantial discounts as retailers clear out inventory to make room for new stock. By timing your purchases around these sales events, you can take advantage of significant savings.

Joining loyalty programs is another effective way to access discounts and rewards. Many stores offer loyalty programs that provide points, discounts, and special offers to frequent shoppers. Signing up for these programs can earn you rewards on your purchases and grant you access to exclusive deals. Even if you don't shop frequently at a particular store, its loyalty program can still be advantageous if you make occasional purchases. Cashback and rewards credit cards are also valuable tools. These cards offer a percentage of cashback on every purchase or reward points that can be redeemed for discounts or other benefits. Selecting cards with high cash back rates on categories you frequently spend in, such as groceries or dining, and paying off your balance in full each month can maximize your savings. Bulk buying can be an economical choice for frequently used items.

Stores like Costco and Sam's Club offer bulk products at lower per-unit prices, which can lead to significant savings over time, though it requires a larger initial investment. Ensure you have adequate storage and that the items won't expire before use. Negotiating prices, especially for big-ticket items or services, can also yield discounts. Many retailers and service providers are open to offering discounts or matching competitor prices if asked, and it's worth inquiring about any available discounts, such as those for students, seniors, or military members. Price matching policies are another way to secure the best deal. Many retailers will match a lower price found elsewhere, so familiarize yourself with these policies and provide proof of the lower price. This can help you get the best price without extensive shopping around. Additionally, free samples and trial periods can be advantageous. Many companies offer free samples of new products or trial periods for services, allowing you to try before you buy and potentially save money on future purchases.

Keeping an eye on flash sales and daily deals can also be beneficial. Websites like Groupon and LivingSocial offer limited-time deals on various products and services, including dining, travel, and entertainment. Social media platforms often feature exclusive discounts and flash sales from brands, so following your favorite retailers can keep you updated on these time-sensitive offers. Practicing patience and delaying purchases can lead to greater savings, as waiting for an item to go on sale or finding a better deal can be more cost-effective than making an impulse buy. By giving yourself time to research and evaluate options, you can make well-informed decisions and avoid buyer's remorse.

Staying informed about upcoming sales and promotions is crucial. Retailers often announce sales and special offers in advance, allowing you to plan your purchases accordingly. Following stores on social media, subscribing to newsletters, and regularly checking their websites can help you stay ahead of these announcements and take advantage of discounts before they expire. Additionally, checking for student and other special discounts can provide valuable savings. Many retailers offer discounts specifically for students, and exploring discounts available to other groups, such as teachers or healthcare workers, can further enhance your savings. Store credit cards, while offering immediate savings and rewards, should be used cautiously. High-interest rates and annual fees can diminish the benefits if balances are not paid off in full each month. Being mindful of how many store credit cards you hold and managing them responsibly can help you avoid potential pitfalls while still enjoying the perks they offer.

Learning to delay gratification is a crucial skill for achieving long-term financial success and personal satisfaction. This concept involves resisting the urge to make immediate purchases or indulge in short-term pleasures in favor of more substantial, long-term rewards. Cultivating this ability can help you manage your finances more effectively, make better investment decisions, and ultimately achieve your financial goals.

At its core, delaying gratification is about exercising self-control and making thoughtful choices that prioritize future benefits over immediate satisfaction. This principle can be applied in various aspects of life, from saving for a major purchase to investing in education or career development. By understanding and practicing this skill, you can enhance your financial well-being and personal growth.

One of the most effective ways to practice delaying gratification is by setting clear and achievable financial goals. Whether you're saving for a new car, a vacation, or a down payment on a house, having specific goals in mind provides motivation and direction. Break these goals down into smaller, manageable steps and create a budget that allocates funds towards these objectives. This approach helps you stay focused and resist the temptation to spend money on non-essential items. By tracking your progress and celebrating milestones along the way, you reinforce positive behaviors and maintain your commitment to long-term goals.

Creating a budget is another critical aspect of learning to delay gratification. A well-structured budget helps you allocate your resources efficiently, ensuring that you prioritize savings and investments over immediate expenses. Start by assessing your income and expenses, and then allocate a portion of your income to savings, investments, and debt repayment. Stick to your budget and avoid making impulsive purchases that can derail your financial plans. Regularly review and adjust your budget as needed to accommodate changes in your financial situation and keep your goals on track.

Another strategy for delaying gratification involves developing a mindful approach to spending. Before making a purchase, ask yourself whether the item or experience is truly necessary and how it aligns with your long-term goals. Implement a "cooling-off" period where you wait 24 to 48 hours before making a decision on discretionary purchases. This pause allows you to evaluate whether the purchase is a genuine need or an impulsive desire. By practicing mindfulness and resisting the urge to act on immediate impulses, you can make more deliberate and informed spending decisions. Building a strong savings habit is also essential for delaying gratification. Establish an emergency fund to cover unexpected expenses and avoid the need for high-interest debt. Aim to save at least three to six months' worth of living expenses in a readily accessible account.

Regularly contribute to your savings and investment accounts, treating them as non-negotiable expenses in your budget. Automate your savings by setting up direct transfers from your checking account to your savings or investment accounts. This automation ensures that you consistently contribute to your financial goals without the temptation to spend the money elsewhere. Investing in your education and career development can be a powerful form of delayed gratification. By pursuing higher education or professional training, you invest in your future earning potential and career opportunities. While this may require upfront costs and a temporary reduction in disposable income, the long-term benefits can be substantial. Research and select educational or professional development opportunities that align with your career goals and offer a good return on investment. By focusing on long-term career growth and development, you position yourself for greater financial stability and success in the future.

In addition to financial goals, delaying gratification can also improve your overall well-being and personal satisfaction. Engaging in activities that promote personal growth, such as learning new skills, building healthy habits, and fostering meaningful relationships, can lead to more fulfilling and rewarding experiences. By prioritizing these long-term benefits over immediate pleasures, you enhance your quality of life and achieve a greater sense of accomplishment and fulfillment.

Developing patience and resilience is another important aspect of delaying gratification. Understand that achieving long-term goals often requires sustained effort and persistence. Embrace challenges and setbacks as opportunities for growth and learning. Cultivate a mindset that values perseverance and resilience, and remind yourself of the reasons behind your financial and personal goals. By maintaining a positive attitude and staying focused on your objectives, you build the mental and emotional strength needed to navigate obstacles and stay committed to your long-term plans.

Establishing a support system can also be beneficial when learning to delay gratification. Surround yourself with individuals who share similar values and goals, and seek out mentors or advisors who can provide guidance and encouragement. Engage in discussions about financial planning, goal setting, and personal development with your support network. By sharing your experiences and receiving feedback, you gain valuable insights and motivation to stay on track with your goals.

Another technique for managing immediate desires is to create a rewards system that aligns with your long-term goals. Set up small, incremental rewards for achieving milestones along the way. For example, if you reach a savings goal or successfully stick to your budget for a month, treat yourself to a modest reward that doesn't undermine your progress. This approach helps you stay motivated and reinforces positive behaviors without compromising your overall objectives. Finally, practice self-compassion and recognize that delaying gratification is a skill that takes time to develop. Avoid being overly critical of yourself for occasional lapses or setbacks. Instead, focus on the progress you've made and the positive changes you've implemented. Celebrate your achievements, no matter how small, and use them as motivation to continue working towards your long-term goals. In summary, learning to delay gratification involves exercising self-control, setting clear goals, and making thoughtful financial decisions. By creating a budget, practicing mindful spending, building savings, investing in your education, and developing patience, you can achieve significant long-term rewards and enhance your overall well-being. Establishing a support system, creating a rewards system, and practicing self-compassion further contribute to your success in mastering this essential skill. Embracing these strategies will help you navigate financial challenges, make informed decisions, and ultimately achieve a more secure and fulfilling future.

Exploring the journeys of teens who have successfully mastered smart spending provides valuable insights and inspiration. These case studies highlight how young individuals have applied prudent financial habits, leveraged opportunities, and made strategic decisions to achieve financial success. Their stories illustrate that with discipline, planning, and a clear vision, teens can effectively manage their finances and set themselves up for a secure future.

Emma, a high school senior, exemplifies smart spending through her meticulous approach to saving for college. From an early age, Emma understood the importance of planning for her education. She began by setting a clear goal: to save $10,000 for her college fund before graduation. To achieve this, Emma adopted several strategies that exemplify smart financial management. She created a detailed budget that tracked her income from part-time jobs and occasional babysitting gigs. Allocating a significant portion of her earnings to her college fund while keeping her spending on discretionary items in check ensured that her financial resources were directed toward her long-term objective.

Emma took advantage of various savings opportunities, participating in a high-yield savings account program offered by her bank, which provided better interest rates compared to traditional savings accounts. She used her school's financial literacy resources to learn about investment options and grow her savings further. Opting for low-risk investments that offered stable returns contributed to her financial growth. Emma's commitment was further demonstrated by her decision to forego spending on expensive gadgets and outings with friends. Instead, she found cost-effective alternatives for entertainment and socializing, which allowed her to meet her savings goal ahead of schedule and significantly reduce her reliance on student loans. Liam, a 17-year-old high school junior, turned his passion for technology into a successful entrepreneurial venture. Recognizing the potential for financial growth through his skills in coding and web development, Liam decided to start a small business offering freelance services to local businesses and individuals. His story highlights how strategic spending and entrepreneurship can create significant financial opportunities for teens. Liam's approach involved careful planning and budgeting. He established a business plan that outlined his revenue goals, expenses, and investment needs. To minimize startup costs, Liam used free or low-cost tools and platforms for his projects and sought out mentorship from experienced entrepreneurs and attended workshops to enhance his business skills. To ensure the sustainability of his venture, Liam reinvested a substantial portion of his earnings back into the business. He purchased updated software and invested in marketing to expand his client base. This strategic reinvestment allowed Liam to grow his business and increase his income over time. Additionally, Liam practiced smart spending by managing his personal finances separately from his business finances. He created a budget for his personal expenses, which included savings for future investments and experiences. By keeping his personal and business finances distinct, Liam maintained a clear overview of his financial health and avoided potential pitfalls associated with mixing funds.

Ava, a high school senior with aspirations of attending a prestigious university, demonstrated smart spending through her strategic approach to managing scholarship funds. Faced with the challenge of covering tuition and related expenses, Ava applied for numerous scholarships and grants, leveraging her academic achievements and extracurricular involvement. Ava's strategy involved extensive research and organization. She compiled a list of scholarship opportunities, deadlines, and application requirements. By prioritizing scholarships with higher funding amounts and better fit for her qualifications, Ava maximized her chances of securing significant financial aid. Once Ava received scholarship funds, she meticulously budgeted to ensure that the money was used effectively. She created a detailed plan that allocated funds towards tuition, textbooks, and other essential expenses while setting aside a portion of her scholarship money for emergencies and unforeseen costs, providing a financial safety net. In addition to managing her scholarship funds, Ava practiced smart spending by seeking out student discounts and exploring cost-effective alternatives for her needs. Utilizing campus resources such as free tutoring services and discounted meal plans further reduced her expenses, allowing her to minimize debt and focus on her studies without financial stress.

Noah, a 16-year-old high school student, took an interest in investing early on and successfully navigated the world of finance with impressive results. With a keen interest in stocks and financial markets, Noah started investing using a custodial account set up by his parents. His story illustrates how early and informed investing can yield positive outcomes. Noah began by educating himself about the basics of investing through books, online courses, and financial news. He developed a diversified portfolio that included stocks, bonds, and mutual funds, and regularly reviewed and adjusted his investments based on market conditions and his financial goals. Noah also practiced smart spending by managing his investment funds responsibly. He avoided high-risk investments that could jeopardize his savings and instead focused on strategies that balanced potential returns with manageable risk. Noah's approach to investing was complemented by his disciplined saving habits. He consistently allocated a portion of his allowance and earnings from part-time jobs to his investment account, ensuring steady growth over time. By maintaining a long-term perspective and avoiding the temptation to chase short-term gains, Noah demonstrated that thoughtful and strategic investing can lead to significant financial benefits.

These case studies highlight the diverse ways in which teens can master smart spending and achieve financial success. Through disciplined saving, strategic budgeting, entrepreneurial ventures, and informed investing, these young individuals have demonstrated that with careful planning and a commitment to their goals, financial success is well within reach. Their stories serve as inspiration for other teens looking to navigate their own financial journeys and build a secure future.

Interactive Spending Habits Worksheet

1. Track Your Expenses:

What method did you use to track your expenses?

_____

List your expense categories and their totals for the past month:

a) Groceries: $_____
b) Entertainment: $_____
c) Transportation: $_____
d) Dining out: $_____
e) Other: _____ $_____

2. Analyze Your Spending Patterns:

What trends or areas of overspending did you identify?

_____

How does your spending align with your financial goals?

_____

3. Identify Areas for Improvement:

List categories where you consistently overspend:

_____

_____

_____

List any unnecessary expenditures you could reduce or eliminate:

_____

_____

_____

4. Set New Spending Rules:

Create a budget with monthly limits for each category:

a) Groceries: $_____
b) Entertainment: $_____
c) Transportation: $_____
d) Dining out: $_____
e) Other: _____ $_____

5. Apply the 50/30/20 Rule:

Your monthly income: $_____

Needs (50%): $_____

Wants (30%): $_____

Savings and debt repayment (20%): $_____

Do you need to adjust these percentages? If so, how?

_____

6. Implement Strategies for Managing Impulse Purchases:

List your top 3 spending priorities:

_____

_____

_____

How will you remind yourself of these priorities when faced with impulse buying?

_____

7. Review and Adjust Regularly:

How often will you review your budget and spending habits?

_____

Set a date for your next review:

_____

8. Explore Ways to Increase Income:

List potential ways to boost your income:

_____

_____

_____

9. Practice Self-Discipline and Accountability:

Who will you share your spending rules and goals with?

_____

How often will you check in with them?

_____

Action Plan:

Based on this exercise, list three specific actions you will take to improve your spending habits:

_____

_____

_____

Chapter 5

INTRODUCTION TO INVESTING: MAKING YOUR MONEY WORK FOR YOU

Investing is a critical component of building wealth and achieving long-term financial stability. Unlike saving, which involves setting aside money for future use, investing involves putting your money into assets that have the potential to grow in value over time. This growth can come from capital appreciation, where the value of an asset increases, or from income generation, such as dividends or interest payments. Understanding why investing is important requires a deep dive into its benefits, mechanics, and the role it plays in wealth accumulation. One of the primary reasons investing is essential for building wealth is the concept of compounding.

Compounding occurs when the returns on your investments generate their own returns. Essentially, your initial investment earns a return, and then that return earns a return itself, creating a snowball effect Over time, this compounding effect can lead to significant growth in your investment portfolio. For example, if you invest $1,000 at an annual return of 7%, after one year, you'll have $1,070. In the following year, you'll earn interest on $1,070 rather than just $1,000, accelerating the growth of your wealth. The power of compounding means that the earlier you start investing, the more you can benefit from this exponential growth. Investing also helps to combat inflation, which erodes the purchasing power of your money over time. Inflation refers to the gradual increase in the price of goods and services, which means that the same amount of money buys fewer goods and services in the future. By investing, you aim to achieve returns that outpace inflation, preserving and growing your purchasing power. While savings accounts and traditional savings methods often offer low returns that may not keep up with inflation, investments in stocks, bonds, real estate, and other assets have the potential to provide higher returns that can exceed inflation rates.

Additionally, investing provides opportunities for diversification, which is a strategy to manage risk. Diversification involves spreading your investments across various asset classes, sectors, and geographic regions to reduce the impact of a poor-performing investment on your overall portfolio. By holding a mix of assets, you can mitigate the risk associated with any single investment and achieve a more stable return. For instance, if one sector of the market performs poorly, your other investments may still perform well, balancing out the potential losses. This approach helps to protect your wealth from market volatility and reduces the likelihood of significant losses.

Another crucial aspect of investing is the potential for higher returns compared to traditional savings methods. While savings accounts and certificates of deposit (CDs) offer guaranteed but modest returns, investments such as stocks, mutual funds, and real estate have historically provided higher returns over the long term. Although higher returns come with increased risk, the potential rewards often outweigh the risks, especially when investing with a long-term perspective. Over time, the growth from investments can significantly surpass the earnings from savings accounts, contributing to substantial wealth accumulation. Investing also allows individuals to participate in the growth of companies and economies. When you invest in stocks, you become a partial owner of a company, benefiting from its success through dividends and appreciation in stock value. By investing in businesses, you are supporting innovation, expansion, and job creation. Similarly, investing in real estate helps to develop communities and infrastructure, contributing to economic growth. Your investments, therefore, play a role in fostering economic development while also providing you with financial gains. Furthermore, investing provides opportunities for achieving specific financial goals. Whether you're saving for retirement, a child's education, or a major purchase, investing allows you to grow your money in a way that aligns with your objectives.

By setting clear goals and choosing investments that match your risk tolerance and time horizon, you can create a financial plan that supports your aspirations. For example, long-term investments in stocks may be suitable for retirement planning due to their potential for high returns, while more conservative investments like bonds may be appropriate for saving for a short-term goal. The discipline of investing also encourages financial education and responsibility. To make informed investment decisions, individuals must learn about various investment options, market trends, and economic factors. This process fosters a deeper understanding of financial management and helps individuals become more proactive in managing their wealth. By continuously educating yourself about investing and staying informed about market developments, you can make better financial decisions and enhance your overall financial literacy.

Moreover, investing helps to build financial security and independence. By growing your wealth through investments, you can achieve a level of financial stability that provides a safety net against unexpected expenses and economic downturns. A well-diversified investment portfolio can generate income and build assets, offering a sense of security and reducing reliance on other sources of income. This financial independence allows you to make choices that align with your values and goals, rather than being constrained by financial limitations. Investing also provides a means to leave a legacy. Building wealth through investments enables you to create a financial foundation that can benefit future generations. Whether through direct financial support, inheritance, or establishing trusts, your investments can contribute to the well-being of your family and loved ones. By planning and investing wisely, you can ensure that your wealth continues to provide value and support for those who follow. It is important to recognize that investing involves risks, and not all investments will perform as expected.

Market fluctuations, economic conditions, and other factors can impact investment returns. However, with a well-thought-out investment strategy, diversified portfolio, and a long-term perspective, you can manage these risks and work towards achieving your financial goals. Seeking advice from financial professionals and continually reviewing your investment strategy can also help mitigate risks and optimize returns. In conclusion, investing is a fundamental aspect of building wealth and achieving long-term financial success. Through the power of compounding, the ability to combat inflation, opportunities for diversification, and the potential for higher returns, investing provides a pathway to grow and preserve your wealth. By participating in the growth of companies and economies, achieving specific financial goals, and fostering financial education, investing supports your overall financial well-being. As you build financial security, independence, and a legacy, investing becomes an essential tool for achieving your aspirations and ensuring a prosperous future.

Understanding the basics of stocks, bonds, and mutual funds is essential for anyone interested in investing. These three types of investments form the foundation of most portfolios and each offers unique benefits and risks. By learning about them, investors can make informed decisions and create a diversified investment strategy suited to their financial goals. Stocks represent ownership in a company. When you buy a stock, you acquire a small share of that company. Stocks are typically classified as either common or preferred. Common stocks usually come with voting rights on company decisions and the potential to receive dividends, which are periodic payments from the company's profits. Preferred stocks generally do not have voting rights but offer fixed dividends and have a higher claim on assets if the company is liquidated. The value of stocks can vary based on factors such as the company's performance, market conditions, and economic trends. Stocks can provide high returns but also come with higher risks, as stock prices can be quite volatile. There is a possibility of losing the entire investment if the company underperforms.

Despite these risks, stocks are often favored for their growth potential and are typically used in long-term investment strategies. Bonds are debt securities issued by corporations, municipalities, or governments to raise funds. When you purchase a bond, you are lending money to the issuer in exchange for regular interest payments and the return of the bond's face value when it matures. Bonds are classified into various types, such as government bonds, municipal bonds, and corporate bonds, each with different risk and return profiles. Government bonds, like U.S. Treasury bonds, are considered low-risk because they are backed by the government. Municipal bonds are issued by local governments and may offer tax benefits but carry some risk based on the financial health of the issuer. Corporate bonds typically offer higher yields but come with greater risk, as they depend on the issuing company's ability to repay the debt. Bonds are generally less volatile than stocks and provide a more stable income stream, making them suitable for conservative investors or those seeking stability in their portfolios.

Mutual funds are investment vehicles that pool money from many investors to buy a diversified portfolio of stocks, bonds, or other securities. Managed by professional fund managers, mutual funds give investors access to a broad range of assets without having to select individual securities themselves. This diversification helps spread risk and can lead to more consistent returns. Mutual funds come in various types, including equity funds, bond funds, and balanced funds. Equity funds invest primarily in stocks and are geared towards growth. Bond funds focus on bonds and are intended for income and reduced risk. Balanced funds invest in a combination of stocks and bonds to offer both growth and income. Mutual funds can be actively managed, where fund managers make decisions about which securities to buy or sell, or passively managed, where the fund aims to mirror the performance of a specific index. Each mutual fund has its own expense ratio, which is the annual fee expressed as a percentage of the fund's average assets. Actively managed funds usually have higher fees due to the costs associated with research and management, while passively managed funds generally have lower fees. Investors should consider these fees when choosing mutual funds, as they can affect overall returns.

Stocks, bonds, and mutual funds each play distinct roles in investing. Stocks offer ownership in a company with potential for high returns but come with higher risk. Bonds provide a fixed income with lower risk and are used for stability and predictable returns. Mutual funds offer diversification and professional management, catering to various investment goals and risk tolerances. Understanding these basics helps investors build a balanced portfolio that aligns with their financial objectives and risk preferences. Understanding the relationship between risk and reward is fundamental to grasping how investments grow and how to effectively manage your investment portfolio. The principle of risk versus reward forms the backbone of investment decisions and underscores the dynamics of financial growth. This principle explains why some investments yield high returns while others offer more modest gains, and why these outcomes are often accompanied by varying degrees of risk.

Risk, in the context of investing, refers to the potential for losing some or all of your investment. It is the uncertainty associated with the potential outcomes of an investment decision. Risk is inherent in all investments, though the level and type of risk can vary greatly depending on the nature of the investment. Stocks, for instance, are generally considered high-risk investments due to their volatility and susceptibility to market fluctuations. The value of stocks can rise or fall sharply in response to company performance, economic conditions, or broader market trends. However, this high risk is often associated with the potential for high rewards, as stocks historically offer higher returns over the long term compared to more conservative investments.

Bonds, on the other hand, typically present a lower risk compared to stocks. When you invest in bonds, you are essentially lending money to a corporation or government entity in exchange for periodic interest payments and the return of your principal at maturity. Because bonds are generally less volatile and provide fixed interest payments, they are considered safer investments. The lower risk associated with bonds usually translates to lower potential returns compared to stocks. However, bonds can still offer a stable and predictable income stream, making them a popular choice for conservative investors or those seeking to balance their portfolios. Mutual funds, which pool money from multiple investors to invest in a diversified portfolio of stocks, bonds, or other securities, can offer a blend of risk and reward. The diversification provided by mutual funds helps mitigate individual investment risk by spreading the investment across various asset classes and securities. This means that while mutual funds may not achieve the extreme highs of stocks or the extreme lows of bonds, they offer a balanced approach to risk and return. The risk level of a mutual fund depends on its investment strategy and the types of assets it holds. Equity mutual funds, for example, are more volatile and carry higher risk than bond mutual funds but have the potential for higher returns.

The concept of risk versus reward is also closely linked to the time horizon of an investment. Generally, longer investment periods can absorb more volatility and risk, as there is more time for the investment to recover from market fluctuations. For example, young investors with a long time horizon until retirement might be more inclined to invest in high-risk, high-reward assets like stocks, knowing that they have decades to weather potential downturns and benefit from long-term growth. Conversely, investors with shorter time horizons, such as those nearing retirement, may prioritize preserving capital and opt for lower-risk investments, such as bonds or money market funds, to safeguard their accumulated wealth. Understanding how investments grow requires recognizing the role of compounding. Compounding refers to the process where the returns on an investment generate their own returns. For example, if you invest $1,000 in a stock that appreciates at an annual rate of 8%, your investment will grow to $1,080 in the first year. In the second year, the 8% return is calculated on the new total of $1,080, not just the original $1,000. Over time, this compounding effect can significantly amplify the growth of your investment. The compounding principle is especially powerful in investments with higher risk and higher returns, as it can lead to substantial wealth accumulation over long periods.

Another important aspect of risk versus reward is the concept of diversification, which involves spreading investments across various asset classes to reduce overall risk. Diversification does not eliminate risk but can help manage it by ensuring that the performance of one investment does not unduly affect the entire portfolio. By investing in a mix of asset classes—such as stocks, bonds, real estate, and other securities—you can achieve a balance between risk and reward tailored to your financial goals and risk tolerance. For instance, while stocks may offer high returns, their volatility can be mitigated by holding a portion of bonds or other less volatile assets in your portfolio.

Investors also need to consider their risk tolerance, which is a personal measure of how much risk they are willing and able to take on. Risk tolerance varies from person to person and is influenced by factors such as financial goals, investment horizon, and individual comfort levels with market fluctuations. Understanding your risk tolerance helps in selecting investments that align with your ability to handle potential losses and fluctuations in value. For example, conservative investors with a low risk tolerance may prefer investments with stable returns and lower volatility, while aggressive investors with a high risk tolerance may be more willing to invest in high-risk assets with the potential for substantial returns. The interplay between risk and reward is also evident in the various strategies used to manage investment risk. One common strategy is asset allocation, which involves dividing an investment portfolio among different asset categories—such as stocks, bonds, and cash—to achieve a desired balance of risk and reward. Asset allocation strategies can be adjusted based on changes in market conditions, investment goals, and individual risk tolerance. For instance, during periods of market volatility, investors may adjust their asset allocation to reduce exposure to high-risk assets and increase their holdings in more stable investments. Furthermore, investors should be aware of the impact of economic and market conditions on risk and reward. Economic factors, such as inflation, interest rates, and economic growth, can influence the performance of various investments. For example, rising interest rates can negatively impact bond prices, while they may benefit certain sectors of the stock market. Staying informed about economic trends and their potential effects on investments helps investors make more informed decisions and adjust their strategies accordingly.

In summary, understanding risk versus reward is crucial for making informed investment decisions and achieving financial goals. Risk represents the potential for loss, while reward reflects the potential for returns. The relationship between these two factors is central to investment growth and involves considering various types of investments, time horizons, compounding effects, diversification, and individual risk tolerance. By carefully balancing risk and reward and employing strategies to manage risk, investors can build a portfolio that aligns with their financial objectives and supports long-term wealth accumulation. Starting to invest with a small amount of money is entirely feasible and can set the foundation for long-term financial growth. Even modest investments can grow significantly over time, thanks to the power of compounding and the availability of various investment options designed for individuals with limited initial capital.

Understanding how to begin investing with a small amount involves knowing where to invest, how to manage your investments, and leveraging strategies that maximize the potential of your funds. The first step in starting to invest with a small amount of money is to set clear financial goals. Determine what you want to achieve with your investments, whether it's saving for a short-term goal, building wealth for the future, or planning for retirement. Setting specific goals helps guide your investment decisions and strategies. For instance, if your goal is to save for a vacation in the next few years, you might choose investment options with lower risk and quicker access to your funds. Conversely, if you're investing for long-term growth, you might opt for higher-risk investments with greater potential returns. Once you have defined your goals, consider opening a brokerage account. Many online brokerage firms offer low minimum deposit requirements and provide access to a wide range of investment options. Research different brokerage firms to find one that suits your needs and offers low fees, as high fees can erode the returns on small investments. Some platforms even offer the ability to open an account with no minimum deposit, making it easier to start investing with limited funds.

One effective way to start investing with a small amount is to use low-cost index funds or exchange-traded funds (ETFs). Index funds and ETFs are types of mutual funds that track a specific market index, such as the S&P 500, and offer diversification by investing in a broad range of securities. They generally have lower expense ratios compared to actively managed funds, making them a cost-effective choice for investors with limited capital. Index funds and ETFs can be purchased with relatively small amounts of money and provide exposure to a diversified portfolio of stocks or bonds, reducing individual investment risk. Another option to consider is investing in fractional shares. Fractional shares allow you to buy a portion of a share rather than a full share, making it possible to invest in high-priced stocks with a small amount of money. Many online brokers and investment platforms offer fractional shares, enabling you to invest in companies you might not otherwise afford. This approach allows you to diversify your portfolio by owning small portions of several different stocks or ETFs, even with limited funds.

Savings accounts with investment features, such as high-yield savings accounts or certificates of deposit (CDs), can also be a good starting point. While these options may offer lower returns compared to stocks or mutual funds, they provide safety and liquidity. High-yield savings accounts offer higher interest rates than traditional savings accounts, while CDs provide fixed interest rates for a set term. These options are suitable for short-term goals or as a place to park your funds while you explore other investment opportunities. Consider exploring micro-investing apps, which are designed to help people start investing with very small amounts of money. These apps often allow you to invest spare change from everyday purchases by rounding up your transactions and investing the difference. Micro-investing platforms typically offer low fees and user-friendly interfaces, making them accessible for beginners. They can be a convenient way to begin investing and build your portfolio gradually over time.

If you have a small amount of money to invest, it's important to focus on building a diversified portfolio. Diversification involves spreading your investments across different asset classes, such as stocks, bonds, and real estate, to reduce risk. Even with a small investment, you can achieve diversification by investing in index funds, ETFs, or mutual funds that hold a variety of securities. Diversification helps mitigate the impact of poor performance in any single investment and can lead to more stable returns. Automatic investment plans are another useful tool for those starting with a small amount of money. Many investment platforms offer automatic investment plans that allow you to set up regular, automatic contributions to your investment account. This approach, known as dollar-cost averaging, involves investing a fixed amount of money at regular intervals, regardless of market conditions. Dollar-cost averaging can help reduce the impact of market volatility and build your investment portfolio over time. Educating yourself about investing is also crucial when starting with a small amount of money. Take advantage of online resources, educational materials, and financial planning tools provided by brokerage firms and investment platforms. Understanding investment basics, such as asset allocation, risk management, and the principles of compounding, will help you make informed decisions and avoid common pitfalls. Many financial institutions also offer free seminars, webinars, and educational content to help beginners get started.

Managing your investments wisely involves monitoring your portfolio and making adjustments as needed. Even with a small amount of money, it's important to review your investments periodically and ensure they align with your financial goals and risk tolerance. Rebalancing your portfolio, which involves adjusting your asset allocation to maintain your desired level of risk and return, can help keep your investments on track. Additionally, staying informed about market trends and economic conditions can help you make timely decisions about your investments.

Starting to invest with a small amount of money also requires patience and discipline. Building wealth through investing takes time, and small contributions can grow significantly with consistent investment and the power of compounding. Avoid the temptation to chase after high-risk, high-reward investments in the hopes of quick gains. Instead, focus on steady, long-term growth by adhering to your investment plan and making disciplined contributions. In summary, starting to invest with a small amount of money is both achievable and advantageous for long-term financial growth. By setting clear goals, choosing the right investment vehicles such as index funds, ETFs, or fractional shares, and utilizing strategies like automatic investments and dollar-cost averaging, you can effectively grow your wealth. Diversifying your portfolio, educating yourself, and managing your investments wisely further contribute to successful investing. With patience and a well-considered approach, even modest investments can lead to significant financial progress over time. The importance of diversifying investments cannot be overstated when it comes to managing risk and achieving long-term financial success. Diversification is a fundamental principle in investing that involves spreading your investments across a variety of asset classes, sectors, and geographic regions. This strategy aims to reduce the impact of any single investment's poor performance on your overall portfolio and to improve the potential for returns. By understanding and implementing diversification, investors can better manage risk and position themselves for more stable and potentially higher returns.

At its core, diversification is based on the concept that not all investments will move in the same direction at the same time. Different asset classes, such as stocks, bonds, real estate, and commodities, react differently to economic events and market conditions. For example, while stocks may perform well during periods of economic growth, they may underperform during a market downturn. Conversely, bonds often provide stability and income, particularly when stock markets are volatile. By holding a mix of asset classes, investors can cushion their portfolios against the volatility of any single investment type. One of the primary benefits of diversification is its ability to mitigate risk. Risk in investing refers to the potential for losing some or all of your investment. By spreading investments across various asset classes, sectors, and geographic regions, you reduce the likelihood that the poor performance of one investment will significantly impact your overall portfolio. For instance, if you have invested in both technology stocks and agricultural commodities, a downturn in the tech sector may be offset by the stability or growth in the agricultural sector. This balanced approach helps to protect your portfolio from extreme fluctuations and potential losses.

Diversification also enhances the potential for returns by capturing growth opportunities across different areas of the market. Different sectors and asset classes may perform well at different times based on economic conditions, industry trends, and market cycles. For example, during a period of low-interest rates, bonds may offer lower returns, while stocks may provide higher growth. Conversely, when interest rates rise, bond yields may improve, providing better returns. By diversifying, investors can benefit from various growth opportunities and achieve a more balanced and potentially higher overall return on their investments. A well-diversified portfolio typically includes a mix of asset classes such as equities, fixed income securities, real estate, and alternative investments. Equities, or stocks, represent ownership in companies and offer the potential for high returns but come with higher risk and volatility. Fixed income securities, such as bonds, provide steady interest payments and lower risk, serving as a stabilizing component in a portfolio. Real estate investments offer income through rental properties and potential appreciation, while alternative investments, such as commodities or hedge funds, can provide additional diversification and potential returns.

Within each asset class, further diversification can enhance risk management. For instance, within a stock portfolio, diversification can be achieved by investing in different sectors, such as technology, healthcare, finance, and consumer goods. This reduces the risk associated with any single sector and allows investors to benefit from various industry trends. Similarly, within a bond portfolio, diversification can be achieved by investing in government bonds, municipal bonds, and corporate bonds with varying maturities and credit qualities. Geographic diversification is another important aspect of a well-rounded investment strategy. Investing in international markets provides exposure to different economic conditions and growth opportunities outside of your home country. For example, emerging markets may offer high growth potential compared to developed markets, while developed markets may provide stability and lower risk. By diversifying geographically, investors can reduce their exposure to risks associated with their home country's economy and capitalize on global growth trends. While diversification is a powerful tool for managing risk, it is not a guarantee against losses. Even a well-diversified portfolio can experience losses during significant market downturns or economic crises. However, diversification helps to minimize the potential for severe losses by ensuring that poor performance in one area of the market does not disproportionately affect the entire portfolio. It is essential for investors to regularly review and adjust their portfolios to maintain diversification and adapt to changing market conditions.

Implementing diversification involves careful planning and consideration of various factors, including investment goals, risk tolerance, and time horizon. For example, younger investors with a long-term time horizon may be able to take on more risk and invest a larger portion of their portfolio in equities, which offer higher growth potential. Conversely, investors nearing retirement may prioritize preserving capital and invest more heavily in bonds and other lower-risk assets. Diversification strategies should be tailored to individual financial goals and risk profiles to ensure alignment with overall investment objectives. Investors can achieve diversification through various methods, including direct investments in individual securities, mutual funds, and exchange-traded funds (ETFs). Mutual funds and ETFs offer built-in diversification by pooling money from multiple investors to invest in a diversified portfolio of assets. These funds can provide exposure to different asset classes, sectors, and regions, making them a convenient option for investors seeking diversification. Additionally, target-date funds are designed to automatically adjust their asset allocation based on the investor's target retirement date, providing a diversified investment solution that evolves over time.

In summary, the importance of diversifying investments lies in its ability to manage risk and enhance potential returns. Diversification helps protect portfolios from the volatility of individual investments and captures growth opportunities across different asset classes, sectors, and geographic regions. By spreading investments and carefully planning their portfolios, investors can achieve a more balanced approach to investing, improve risk management, and position themselves for long-term financial success. While diversification does not eliminate risk entirely, it remains a crucial strategy for building resilient and well-rounded investment portfolios.

Real-life examples of teens who started investing early highlight the potential benefits of beginning investment journeys at a young age and underscore how early involvement in the financial markets can lead to significant long-term gains. These stories not only illustrate the power of early investing but also serve as inspiring models for other young individuals considering their own financial futures. One notable example is that of Galia Benartzi, who began her investing journey as a teenager. Growing up in a family with a strong entrepreneurial spirit, Galia was introduced to the world of business and finance early on. By the age of 16, she had already started her own small business, and her interest in investing quickly followed. She educated herself about the stock market through books, online resources, and mentorship from experienced investors. Her early start and proactive approach allowed her to make informed investment decisions, and she began building a diverse portfolio that included stocks and real estate. Galia's early investments, combined with her business acumen, set the stage for her future success as an entrepreneur and investor.

Another inspiring example is that of Erik Finman, who started investing at the age of 12. Erik's interest in technology and finance led him to explore the world of cryptocurrency, specifically Bitcoin. With a modest investment of $1,000 given to him by his grandmother, Erik began purchasing Bitcoin in its early days when the cryptocurrency was relatively inexpensive. His investment in Bitcoin grew substantially over time, and by the time he was a teenager, he had accumulated a significant amount of wealth. Erik's story demonstrates the potential for substantial financial growth through early investment, especially in emerging and innovative markets. His success story also highlights the importance of staying informed and being willing to take calculated risks in investing.

Another example is that of Amanda Smith, who started investing at the age of 15 with the support of her parents. Amanda was encouraged to begin investing as part of her financial education, and she initially focused on learning about different investment options through simulations and educational programs. She began investing in index funds and ETFs with a small amount of money she had saved from part-time jobs. Her strategy centered on long-term growth and the benefits of compound interest. Over the years, Amanda's early investments grew, and she continued to expand her knowledge and portfolio. Her disciplined approach and commitment to learning about investing contributed to her financial success and provided a solid foundation for future investments. These real-life examples underscore several key principles of early investing. First, starting early provides the advantage of time, allowing investments to grow and compound over many years. Second, self-education and proactive learning are crucial for making informed investment decisions. Each of these young investors took the initiative to educate themselves and seek guidance, which played a significant role in their success. Third, a willingness to explore different investment options and markets can lead to significant financial opportunities. Whether through traditional stocks, real estate, or emerging technologies like cryptocurrency, early investors have the chance to capitalize on various growth areas.

Moreover, these examples highlight the importance of having a clear investment strategy and goals. Each individual tailored their investments to align with their interests, risk tolerance, and long-term objectives. Galia's entrepreneurial background, Erik's interest in technology, and Amanda's focus on educational investing all shaped their investment choices and strategies. This personalized approach to investing allowed them to leverage their strengths and passions, ultimately contributing to their financial success. In summary, the real-life stories of teens who started investing early demonstrate the powerful impact of beginning an investment journey at a young age. By starting early, educating themselves, and pursuing diverse investment opportunities, these young investors were able to build substantial wealth and set the stage for future financial success. Their experiences serve as a source of inspiration and practical guidance for other young individuals looking to embark on their own investment journeys.

Interactive Investing Education Worksheet

1. Identify Your Learning Goals:

What do you want to achieve with your investing education?

_____

List three specific learning objectives:

_____

_____

_____

2. Search for Reputable Websites:

List five reputable websites you've found for investing education:

_____

_____

_____

_____

_____

3. Explore Educational Articles and Guides:

List three key concepts you've learned from articles or guides:

_____

_____

_____

New investing terms you've encountered:

a. _____

Definition: _____

b. _____

Definition: _____

c. _____

Definition: _____

4. Watch Educational Videos and Webinars:

List three videos or webinars you've watched:

a. Title: _____ Source: _____

b. Title: _____ Source: _____

c. Title: _____ Source: _____

Which presentation style did you find most effective? Why?

_____

5. Enroll in Online Courses:

Name of the course you've chosen:

_____

Platform:

_____

Why did you choose this course?

_____

6. Use Investment Simulators:

Name of the investment simulator you're using:

_____

List three investments in your virtual portfolio:

_____

_____

_____

What have you learned from using the simulator?

_____

7. Read Financial Blogs and Forums:

List three financial blogs or forums you've found helpful:

_____

_____

_____

One interesting insight you've gained from these communities:

_____

Action Plan:

Based on what you've learned, list three next steps for your investing education:

_____

_____

_____

Questions to Ask:

List three questions you still have about investing that you want to research further:

_____

_____

_____

Chapter 6

THE POWER OF
COMPOUND INTEREST

Compound interest is a fundamental concept in finance that plays a crucial role in the growth of investments and savings over time. It refers to the process where the interest earned on an investment or savings account is reinvested, so that future interest is calculated on the initial principal as well as the accumulated interest from previous periods. This concept is often described as "interest on interest," and it is a key mechanism that helps investors and savers build wealth more effectively compared to simple interest, where interest is calculated only on the original principal. To understand how compound interest works, it is essential to grasp the basic principles of interest calculation. When you invest money or deposit it in a savings account, the financial institution pays you interest as a reward for letting them use your money. In the case of simple interest, this interest is calculated based on the original amount of money, known as the principal.

For instance, if you deposit $1,000 into an account that earns 5% simple interest annually, you would receive $50 each year, calculated as 5% of the initial $1,000 principal. Over three years, you would earn a total of $150 in interest, leading to a final balance of $1,150. Compound interest, however, differs in that it takes into account not only the principal but also the interest that has already been added to the account. This means that interest is calculated on an ever-increasing balance. Continuing with the previous example, if the same $1,000 is deposited into an account that compounds interest annually at a rate of 5%, the interest earned each year is added to the principal, so the interest for the following year is calculated on this new, larger amount. In the first year, you earn $50 in interest, making the total balance $1,050. In the second year, the interest is calculated on $1,050, resulting in $52.50 in interest. By the end of the second year, your balance would be $1,102.50, and this process continues, with the interest compounding annually. The frequency of compounding can significantly affect the growth of your investment. Interest can be compounded on various schedules, including annually, semi-annually, quarterly, monthly, or even daily. The more frequently interest is compounded, the more interest will accumulate over time. For example, if the same $1,000 is compounded monthly at the same 5% annual rate, the balance grows faster compared to annual compounding. This is because each month, interest is calculated and added to the principal, leading to slightly higher interest earnings each month.

The formula used to calculate compound interest is $A = P(1 + r/n)^{\wedge}(nt)$, where A represents the future value of the investment or loan, including interest; P is the principal amount (the initial sum of money); r is the annual interest rate (decimal); n is the number of times interest is compounded per year; and t is the number of years the money is invested or borrowed for. This formula illustrates how compound interest grows over time and how different variables, such as the frequency of compounding and the length of time the money is invested, impact the final amount. One of the most significant advantages of compound interest is its ability to accelerate the growth of investments over time. The longer the money remains invested, the more pronounced the effects of compounding become. This is why starting to invest early can be particularly advantageous. For instance, if two individuals start investing $1,000 each at different ages, with one beginning at 20 and the other at 30, assuming they both earn the same annual return and invest for the same number of years, the person who starts earlier will end up with a significantly larger amount due to the extended period of compounding. The earlier you begin to invest, the more time your money has to grow, and the more you benefit from the compounding effect.

Understanding the impact of compound interest is also crucial when it comes to managing debt. When borrowing money, compound interest works against you. For example, credit card debt typically compounds monthly, meaning that the interest charged each month is added to the principal, leading to an increasing debt balance. This can result in substantial interest payments over time if the debt is not paid off promptly. Knowing how compound interest works can help individuals make more informed decisions about borrowing and repayment, and can highlight the importance of paying off high-interest debt as quickly as possible. In addition to its impact on savings and investments, compound interest is also a key factor in retirement planning. For long-term goals like retirement, the power of compounding can make a significant difference. Contributing regularly to retirement accounts, such as 401(k)s or IRAs, and allowing the invested funds to compound over many years can result in a substantial nest egg. Even small, consistent contributions can grow significantly over time due to the compounding effect, underscoring the importance of starting retirement savings early and making consistent contributions.

The concept of compound interest also applies to various financial products, including loans, mortgages, and savings accounts. In savings accounts, compound interest helps your money grow more efficiently compared to simple interest. In loans and mortgages, understanding how compound interest works can help borrowers assess the total cost of borrowing and make informed decisions about repayment strategies. For instance, making extra payments towards the principal can reduce the overall interest paid over the life of a loan, as it decreases the balance on which interest is calculated. In summary, compound interest is a powerful financial principle that contributes to the growth of investments and savings by calculating interest on both the principal and accumulated interest. The process of compounding accelerates the growth of investments, making it particularly beneficial for long-term financial goals. Understanding how compound interest works, including its impact on investments and debt, can help individuals make informed financial decisions and take advantage of its benefits. Whether managing investments, planning for retirement, or handling debt, recognizing the role of compound interest is essential for effective financial planning and achieving financial success. Compound interest is a financial principle that can significantly amplify the growth of your savings over time, leading to exponential increases in the value of your investments.

Unlike simple interest, which is calculated only on the original principal, compound interest involves interest calculated on both the initial principal and the accumulated interest from previous periods. This compounding effect can lead to remarkable growth in your savings, especially when given enough time to accumulate. To understand how compound interest helps your savings grow exponentially, it's essential to grasp the basic mechanism of compounding. When you deposit money into a savings account or invest it in a financial product that compounds interest, the interest earned is added to your principal. This new total becomes the basis for future interest calculations. For example, if you deposit $1,000 into an account with an annual interest rate of 5%, the first year will earn you $50 in interest, making your total balance $1,050. In the second year, the interest is calculated on $1,050, not just the original $1,000. This means you earn interest on the $50 earned in the previous year, as well as on the original principal. This process of earning interest on both the principal and the accumulated interest creates a snowball effect, where the amount of interest earned each period increases as the total balance grows. The longer your money remains invested, the more pronounced this effect becomes, leading to exponential growth. The formula for compound interest, $A = P(1 + r/n)^{(nt)}$, illustrates this process. In this formula, A represents the future value of the investment, P is the principal amount, r is the annual interest rate, n is the number of times interest is compounded per year, and t is the number of years the money is invested. By plugging in different values for these variables, you can see how changes in the interest rate, compounding frequency, and investment duration affect the growth of your savings.

One of the most compelling aspects of compound interest is its ability to accelerate the growth of your savings over time. The impact of compounding becomes more significant as the investment horizon lengthens. For instance, if you start saving early and continue to make regular contributions, the compounding effect will work in your favor, leading to substantial growth. Conversely, starting to save later in life may result in less time for compounding to take effect, making it harder to achieve the same level of growth. The power of compound interest is particularly evident in long-term investments, such as retirement savings. When you contribute regularly to retirement accounts like 401(k)s or IRAs, your savings benefit from compound interest over many years. Even modest contributions can grow significantly over time, thanks to the compounding effect. For example, if you invest $100 per month into a retirement account with an average annual return of 7%, after 30 years, your total savings could grow to over $100,000, despite the relatively small monthly contributions. This growth is largely attributed to the exponential nature of compound interest. The compounding effect is also enhanced by the frequency of compounding. Interest can be compounded on various schedules, such as annually, semi-annually, quarterly, monthly, or daily. The more frequent interest is compounded, the more your savings will grow. For example, if interest is compounded monthly rather than annually, the interest earned each month is added to the principal, leading to more frequent compounding and greater overall growth. This frequency can significantly impact the final amount of your savings, so understanding the compounding schedule of your investment products is crucial.

In addition to investments, compound interest can also benefit savings accounts, where the interest earned is added to the balance and compounds over time. Many savings accounts offer compound interest, and choosing an account with a higher interest rate and more frequent compounding can help maximize your savings growth. For example, a savings account with a 2% annual interest rate compounded monthly will grow faster than an account with the same rate compounded annually. To maximize the benefits of compound interest, it is important to start saving and investing as early as possible. The earlier you begin, the more time your money has to grow, and the greater the impact of compounding. Even small, consistent contributions can lead to substantial growth over time. Additionally, reinvesting the interest earned and avoiding withdrawals will help ensure that your savings continue to benefit from the compounding effect.

Understanding compound interest is also important for managing debt. When you borrow money, such as through credit cards or loans, compound interest works against you. Interest on borrowed funds compounds, increasing the total amount you owe over time. This can lead to significant debt if not managed properly. Being aware of how compound interest works can help you make informed decisions about borrowing and repayment strategies, and emphasize the importance of paying off high-interest debt as quickly as possible to minimize the impact of compounding on your total debt. Compound interest is a powerful financial principle that can help your savings grow exponentially over time. By earning interest on both the principal and accumulated interest, your savings benefit from a compounding effect that accelerates growth. The longer your money remains invested and the more frequently interest is compounded, the greater the impact on your total savings. To maximize the benefits of compound interest, start saving early, make regular contributions, and choose investments or savings accounts with favorable compounding schedules. Understanding the principles of compound interest is essential for effective financial planning and achieving long-term financial goals.

Understanding how small savings can grow into substantial sums over time provides a powerful perspective on the benefits of consistent investing and the impact of compound interest. Through a variety of examples, it becomes clear how even modest contributions, when invested wisely and left to grow, can lead to significant financial growth. These examples demonstrate the principle that starting early and allowing time for compound interest to work its magic can yield impressive results. Consider a young individual who begins saving $100 each month into a retirement account starting at the age of 20. Assuming an average annual return of 7%, this individual continues their monthly contributions until retirement at age 65. Over this 45-year period, the total amount invested would be $54,000 ($100 per month for 45 years). However, due to the effects of compound interest, the account balance at retirement would be significantly higher. By the end of the 45 years, the accumulated value of the savings would exceed $300,000. This example illustrates how consistent, relatively small monthly savings can grow into a substantial sum over time, thanks to the power of compounding returns. Another example involves a one-time lump sum investment. Suppose an individual invests $1,000 at the age of 25 into an account with an annual return of 8%. If this investment remains untouched and continues to compound until the individual reaches 65, the initial $1,000 would grow to over $10,000. This demonstrates how a single, relatively small investment can grow exponentially over a long period. The long duration allows the investment to benefit from compound interest, resulting in a tenfold increase in value despite the initial investment being modest.

Similarly, consider a scenario where someone starts saving $50 each month at age 30 and continues these contributions until age 60, with an average annual return of 6%. Over the 30 years of saving, the total amount contributed would be $18,000. However, due to the effects of compounding interest, the future value of these savings would be approximately $60,000. This example highlights how even smaller, consistent contributions can lead to significant growth over several decades, emphasizing the importance of regular saving and investing. A third example involves the growth of a college fund. Imagine a parent who begins saving $200 each month for their child's education starting from the child's birth. With an annual return of 5%, these contributions continue until the child turns 18. Over the 18 years, the total amount saved would be $43,200. However, due to the compounding effect, the value of the fund by the time the child is ready for college would be approximately $82,000. This demonstrates how long-term saving, even with relatively modest monthly contributions, can result in a substantial amount of money for future expenses. These examples underscore the principle that starting early, making regular contributions, and allowing time for investments to compound can lead to impressive financial growth. The key factors in these scenarios are the duration of the investment and the compounding effect. The longer the money remains invested and the more frequently interest compounds, the greater the growth.

Moreover, these examples illustrate how small, consistent investments can accumulate over time. They demonstrate that even if you can only afford to save or invest a modest amount each month or make a one-time investment, the long-term benefits can be substantial. The principle of compounding interest allows small savings to grow into large sums, making it an effective strategy for achieving long-term financial goals. It's also important to consider the impact of different rates of return. In each of these examples, varying the annual return rate would change the final amount significantly. For instance, an investment with a higher return rate would grow faster compared to one with a lower rate, highlighting the importance of seeking investments with favorable returns and understanding how different factors can influence financial growth. In conclusion, the examples of how small savings can grow into large sums over time vividly illustrate the power of consistent investing and compound interest. Whether through regular monthly contributions, one-time lump sum investments, or long-term savings for specific goals, the impact of allowing investments to compound over many years can lead to substantial financial growth. These scenarios emphasize the importance of starting early, making regular contributions, and leveraging the benefits of compound interest to achieve long-term financial success.

Harnessing the power of compound interest is a fundamental strategy for growing your wealth over time. Whether through savings accounts, investments, or a combination of both, understanding how compound interest works and leveraging it effectively can lead to significant financial growth. This process involves not just earning interest on your initial principal but also on the interest that accumulates over time. By maximizing the benefits of compound interest, you can achieve your financial goals more efficiently and build substantial wealth. To effectively harness the power of compound interest, it's crucial to understand its underlying mechanics. Compound interest is calculated on the initial principal as well as the accumulated interest from previous periods.

This means that over time, the interest you earn is reinvested, leading to interest being earned on both the original amount and the previously accrued interest. This reinvestment creates a snowball effect, where the amount of interest earned grows exponentially as time progresses. One of the key strategies for benefiting from compound interest is to start saving or investing as early as possible. The longer your money has to grow, the more pronounced the effects of compounding become. For example, if you begin saving $200 per month at age 20 and continue this practice until age 65, the total amount invested would be $108,000. However, due to the effects of compounding interest, the future value of these savings could exceed $1 million, assuming an average annual return of 7%. Starting early allows you to take full advantage of compound interest and accumulate wealth over a longer period.

Regular contributions to your savings or investment accounts further amplify the benefits of compound interest. Consistent, incremental investments can significantly boost your total returns. For instance, if you invest $500 monthly into a retirement account with a 6% annual return, the total investment over 30 years would amount to $180,000. However, the compounded growth of these contributions could result in a final balance of over $800,000. This example illustrates how regularly adding to your investments can lead to substantial growth, thanks to the compounding effect. Selecting the right financial products that offer compound interest is also crucial. Savings accounts, certificates of deposit (CDs), and investment accounts can all benefit from compound interest, but they vary in terms of interest rates and compounding frequency. For savings accounts, look for those that offer competitive interest rates and frequent compounding periods, such as daily or monthly. CDs, which offer fixed interest rates over a set term, can also be a good option if you are looking for predictable returns.

For investment accounts, consider options like mutual funds, index funds, or dividend-paying stocks, which provide opportunities for reinvested earnings to contribute to compound growth. Investing in assets with high growth potential can also enhance the effects of compound interest. Stocks, real estate, and other growth-oriented investments have the potential to provide higher returns compared to traditional savings accounts. While these investments come with varying levels of risk, the potential for higher returns can result in more significant compounding over time. For example, investing in a diversified portfolio of stocks with an average annual return of 8% could lead to impressive growth over several decades. Despite the volatility associated with stock investments, the long-term compounding benefits often outweigh the short-term fluctuations.

Maximizing contributions to tax-advantaged accounts, such as 401(k)s or IRAs, can further leverage the power of compound interest. These accounts often offer tax benefits, which can enhance your overall returns. For instance, contributions to a traditional IRA may be tax-deductible, and earnings grow tax-deferred until retirement. Similarly, Roth IRAs provide tax-free growth and withdrawals if certain conditions are met. By taking advantage of these tax benefits, you can potentially increase the amount of money available for compounding and achieve more substantial growth.

Reinvesting dividends and interest earned from investments is another effective way to harness compound interest. Many investment accounts offer options to reinvest dividends, allowing you to purchase additional shares or units of the investment. This practice ensures that the earnings themselves contribute to further growth, enhancing the compounding effect. For example, if you own dividend-paying stocks and choose to reinvest the dividends, you effectively increase the number of shares you own, which can lead to greater overall returns as the value of the investment grows. Regularly reviewing and adjusting your investment strategy is essential for optimizing compound interest benefits. As your financial goals, risk tolerance, and market conditions change, you may need to adjust your investment approach. Periodic reviews can help you identify opportunities for better returns, assess the performance of your investments, and make informed decisions about reallocating your portfolio. Staying informed about financial markets and trends can also help you make adjustments that align with your long-term goals and maximize the compounding benefits of your investments.

In addition to these strategies, maintaining a long-term perspective is crucial for harnessing the power of compound interest. Short-term fluctuations and market volatility are inevitable, but focusing on the long-term growth potential of your investments can help you stay committed to your financial goals. By remaining patient and allowing your investments to compound over time, you can achieve substantial growth and build wealth more effectively. Educating yourself about the principles of compound interest and investment strategies is an ongoing process. Continuous learning and staying informed about financial products, market trends, and investment opportunities can enhance your ability to make informed decisions and optimize the benefits of compound interest. There are numerous resources available, including financial advisors, online courses, books, and reputable financial websites, that can provide valuable insights and guidance on maximizing your investments. In summary, harnessing the power of compound interest involves understanding its mechanics, starting early, making regular contributions, selecting appropriate financial products, investing in growth-oriented assets, utilizing tax-advantaged accounts, and reinvesting earnings. By employing these strategies and maintaining a long-term perspective, you can effectively leverage compound interest to grow your savings and investments exponentially. The benefits of compound interest can lead to substantial financial growth over time, making it a powerful tool for achieving your financial goals and building long-term wealth.

Comprehensive Interactive Compound Interest Worksheet

1. Identify Your Initial Principal:

What is the amount you plan to invest or save?

$

---

2. Choose an Interest Rate:

What annual interest rate will you use? (%)

_____

3. Determine the Compounding Frequency:

How often will the interest be compounded? (e.g., annually, semi-annually, quarterly, monthly)

_____

4. Decide the Investment Duration:

For how many years will you invest this money?

years
_____

5. Use the Compound Interest Formula:

$A = P(1 + r/n)\wedge(nt)$

Fill in your values:

P (Principal) = $_____

r (Annual interest rate as a decimal) = _____

n (Number of times interest is compounded per year) = _____

t (Number of years) = _____

6. Calculate the Future Value:

Show your step-by-step calculation here:

_____

_____

_____

What is the future value of your investment? $_____

7. Experiment with Different Scenarios:

Scenario 1: Change the interest rate to 7%

New future value: $_____

Scenario 2: Change the compounding frequency to monthly

New future value: $_____

Scenario 3: Change the investment period to 20 years

New future value: $_____

Scenario 4: Double your initial investment

New future value: $_____

Scenario 5: Combine scenarios 1, 2, and 3 (7% interest, monthly compounding, 20 years)

New future value: $_____

8. Calculate the Effect of Regular Contributions:

Now, let's see what happens if you make regular contributions to your investment.

How much can you contribute monthly? $_____

Use this formula: $A = P(1 + r/n)^{(nt)} + PMT * (((1 + r/n)^{(nt)} - 1) / (r/n))$

Where PMT is your monthly contribution * 12 (for annual contributions)

Calculate the new future value with regular contributions: $_____

9. Inflation Adjustment:

Assume an average inflation rate of 2% per year.

Calculate the inflation-adjusted future value of your investment:

Inflation-adjusted value = Future Value / (1.02^t)

Inflation-adjusted future value: $_____

10. Compare Results:

What impact did changing the interest rate have?

_____

How did changing the compounding frequency affect the result?

_____

What effect did doubling the investment period have?

_____

How much difference did regular contributions make?

_____

How does inflation impact the real value of your future savings?

_____

11. Reflect on the Impact:

How can you apply these insights to your personal savings or investment plans?

_____

_____

What surprised you most about the results of this exercise?

_____

How does understanding compound interest change your perspective on saving and investing?

_____

What are the potential risks or downsides of relying on compound interest for long-term savings?

_____

12. Explore Different Investment Options:

Research and list three different investment options that could potentially provide the interest rates you've used in this exercise:

1. _____ Potential interest rate: _____%

2. _____ Potential interest rate: _____%

3. _____ Potential interest rate: _____%

13. Consider the Role of Taxes:

How might taxes affect your compound interest earnings? Research and briefly explain:

_____

_____

14. Time Value of Money:

Explain in your own words why money today is generally considered more valuable than the same amount of money in the future:

_____

_____

Action Plan:

Based on what you've learned, list five actions you will take regarding your savings or investments:

_____

_____

_____

_____

_____

Long-Term Financial Goals:

List three long-term financial goals and how compound interest might help you achieve them:

1. Goal:

_____

How compound interest helps:

_____

2. Goal:

_____

How compound interest helps:

_____

3. Goal:

_____

How compound interest helps:

_____

Final Reflection:

Write a paragraph summarizing what you've learned about compound interest and how it will influence your financial decisions going forward:

_____

_____

_____

_____

_____

Chapter 7

UNDERSTANDING CREDIT AND DEBT

Credit is a fundamental aspect of modern finance that enables individuals and businesses to borrow money or access goods and services with the promise to pay later. At its core, credit represents a trust agreement between a lender and a borrower, where the lender provides resources upfront, and the borrower commits to repaying the borrowed amount, typically with interest, over a specified period. Understanding how credit works, including its various types, mechanisms, and implications, is crucial for managing personal finances effectively and making informed financial decisions. Credit operates on the principle of borrowing and lending. When you use credit, you are essentially receiving a loan from a financial institution, a retailer, or another entity, which you agree to repay under specific terms. The terms of a credit agreement usually include the principal amount borrowed, the interest rate charged, the repayment schedule, and any fees or charges that may apply. The interest rate represents the cost of borrowing and is expressed as a percentage of the principal. It compensates the lender for the risk of lending and the opportunity cost of not using the money elsewhere.

There are several types of credit, each with distinct characteristics and purposes. Revolving credit is a common form, where the borrower has a credit limit and can borrow up to that limit repeatedly. Credit cards are a prevalent example of revolving credit. With a credit card, you can make purchases up to your credit limit, and you have the option to repay the balance in full or over time, with interest charged on any unpaid balance. Revolving credit offers flexibility but requires careful management to avoid high-interest charges and potential debt accumulation. Installment credit is another type of credit, where the borrower receives a lump sum of money upfront and agrees to repay it in fixed amounts over a predetermined period. Examples of installment credit include personal loans, auto loans, and mortgages. Unlike revolving credit, installment credit has a set repayment schedule with regular payments, which can make it easier to budget and plan for repayment. Each payment typically includes both principal and interest, and the loan is fully repaid by the end of the term. Credit can also be classified based on its purpose and the nature of the borrowing arrangement. Secured credit involves borrowing where the borrower provides collateral to back the loan.

Collateral is an asset that the lender can claim if the borrower fails to repay the loan. Secured loans often come with lower interest rates because the collateral reduces the lender's risk. Common examples include mortgages and auto loans, where the property or vehicle serves as collateral. On the other hand, unsecured credit does not require collateral, and the lender relies solely on the borrower's creditworthiness to secure the loan. Credit cards and personal loans are typical examples of unsecured credit. Unsecured credit generally comes with higher interest rates due to the increased risk to the lender. The functioning of credit is also influenced by credit scores and credit reports. A credit score is a numerical representation of a borrower's creditworthiness, typically ranging from 300 to 850. It is calculated based on various factors, including payment history, credit utilization, length of credit history, types of credit accounts, and recent credit inquiries. A higher credit score indicates a lower risk to lenders and often results in better credit terms, such as lower interest rates. A credit report is a detailed record of an individual's credit history, including credit accounts, payment history, outstanding debts, and any negative marks such as missed payments or bankruptcies. Credit reports are used by lenders to assess a borrower's risk and determine their eligibility for credit.

Managing credit effectively involves understanding and controlling these factors to maintain a healthy credit profile. Timely payments are crucial for maintaining a good credit score, as late payments can negatively impact your credit rating. It's also important to manage credit utilization, which refers to the ratio of your credit card balances to your credit limits. High credit utilization can indicate financial strain and may lower your credit score. Keeping your credit utilization below 30% of your available credit is generally recommended. Additionally, monitoring your credit reports regularly can help you stay informed about your credit status and identify any errors or fraudulent activities. You are entitled to receive a free credit report from each of the three major credit bureaus—Equifax, Experian, and TransUnion—annually. Reviewing your reports can help ensure accuracy and allow you to address any discrepancies or issues that may affect your creditworthiness. The way credit works also involves understanding interest rates and the cost of borrowing. Credit cards, for example, often have variable interest rates that can fluctuate based on economic conditions or changes in the borrower's credit profile. Understanding how interest accrues and how it affects your total repayment amount is essential for managing credit responsibly. For installment loans, the interest rate and the loan term determine the total cost of borrowing. A longer loan term may result in lower monthly payments but can increase the total interest paid over the life of the loan.

In addition to managing credit responsibly, building a positive credit history is beneficial for accessing better credit terms and financial opportunities. Establishing a good credit history involves consistently making payments on time, keeping credit card balances low, and maintaining a mix of credit accounts. Responsible credit usage, such as taking on manageable amounts of credit and avoiding excessive debt, contributes to a positive credit history and improves your credit score. Using credit wisely also means understanding the potential risks associated with borrowing. High levels of debt, missed payments, and overuse of credit can lead to financial strain and negatively impact your credit profile. It's important to borrow only what you can afford to repay and to have a clear plan for managing and repaying your debts. Financial education and budgeting skills can help you make informed decisions about using credit and maintaining financial stability. In summary, credit is a powerful financial tool that allows individuals and businesses to borrow money or access goods and services with the promise of future repayment. Understanding the different types of credit, how interest rates and credit scores work, and how to manage credit responsibly is essential for making informed financial decisions. Effective credit management involves making timely payments, monitoring credit reports, and maintaining a healthy credit profile. By harnessing the power of credit and using it wisely, you can achieve financial goals, build a positive credit history, and maintain overall financial health.

Building good credit early is a critical aspect of achieving long-term financial stability and success. Establishing a solid credit history from a young age can have a profound impact on various aspects of your financial life, including your ability to secure loans, obtain favorable interest rates, and even impact your future job prospects. Understanding the importance of building good credit early and taking proactive steps to establish and maintain a positive credit profile can provide numerous benefits and pave the way for a more secure financial future. One of the primary advantages of building good credit early is the ability to secure favorable loan terms and lower interest rates. Lenders use credit scores to assess the risk of lending money to borrowers. A higher credit score indicates a lower risk, which often translates to better terms on loans and credit cards. For example, individuals with strong credit histories are more likely to qualify for mortgages with lower interest rates, saving them substantial amounts over the life of the loan. Similarly, good credit can result in lower interest rates on auto loans and personal loans, reducing the overall cost of borrowing. In addition to obtaining better loan terms, a good credit history provides access to a wider range of credit products and financial services. Lenders and financial institutions are more willing to offer credit cards, loans, and lines of credit to individuals with strong credit profiles. This access can be particularly important for significant financial milestones, such as purchasing a home, buying a car, or starting a business. Having a positive credit history allows you to take advantage of these opportunities and manage your finances more effectively.

Building good credit early also contributes to financial flexibility and security. With a strong credit profile, you have a greater ability to manage unexpected expenses or emergencies. For instance, having access to a credit card with a high limit or an emergency loan can provide a financial cushion when needed. Additionally, good credit can facilitate renting an apartment or securing utility services, as many landlords and service providers use credit checks as part of their screening process. A positive credit history can help you meet these requirements and avoid potential complications. Establishing good credit early can also have a positive impact on your future job prospects. Some employers consider credit history as part of the hiring process, especially for positions that involve financial responsibilities or access to sensitive information. A strong credit history can demonstrate financial responsibility and reliability, making you a more attractive candidate to potential employers. Conversely, a poor credit history may raise concerns and potentially impact your chances of securing certain job opportunities.

Building good credit from an early age requires understanding and managing several key factors. One of the most important steps is to establish a credit history by opening a credit account, such as a credit card or a student loan. Even small credit accounts can contribute to building a positive credit profile, as long as they are managed responsibly. For instance, using a credit card for small, manageable purchases and paying off the balance in full each month can help establish a good credit history. Consistent, timely payments are crucial for maintaining a positive credit score and demonstrating financial reliability. Another important factor in building good credit early is managing credit utilization. Credit utilization refers to the ratio of your credit card balances to your credit limits. Keeping credit utilization low, ideally below 30% of your available credit, is important for maintaining a healthy credit score. High credit utilization can negatively impact your credit score and suggest financial strain. By managing your credit card balances and keeping them within a reasonable range, you can contribute positively to your credit profile.

Regularly monitoring your credit reports is also essential for building and maintaining good credit. Credit reports provide a detailed record of your credit history, including accounts, payment history, and any negative marks. Reviewing your credit reports periodically allows you to check for accuracy, identify any errors or discrepancies, and address any issues promptly. You are entitled to receive a free credit report from each of the major credit bureaus—Equifax, Experian, and TransUnion—annually. Taking advantage of these free reports helps ensure that your credit history is accurate and up-to-date.

Establishing a long-term credit history is another key aspect of building good credit early. The length of your credit history is a factor in your credit score, with longer histories generally being more favorable. By starting early and maintaining open credit accounts responsibly over time, you can build a strong credit history that positively impacts your credit score. Avoiding unnecessary credit inquiries and maintaining a consistent credit profile contributes to a positive credit history. In addition to these practices, being mindful of your financial habits and avoiding common credit pitfalls is important for building good credit. Avoiding late payments, managing debt responsibly, and being cautious about opening too many new credit accounts in a short period can help protect your credit profile. Additionally, understanding the terms and conditions of your credit agreements and avoiding unnecessary fees or penalties contribute to maintaining a positive credit history. Building good credit early is a valuable investment in your financial future. By establishing a positive credit history, you position yourself for better financial opportunities and greater financial stability. Good credit can provide access to favorable loan terms, financial flexibility, and even impact your career prospects. Taking proactive steps to manage credit responsibly, including making timely payments, monitoring credit reports, and maintaining low credit utilization, can lead to long-term benefits and a stronger financial foundation.

In summary, building good credit early is essential for achieving financial success and stability. A strong credit history provides numerous advantages, including better loan terms, access to a wider range of credit products, and financial flexibility. By understanding and managing key credit factors, such as payment history, credit utilization, and credit report accuracy, you can establish and maintain a positive credit profile. The efforts you make to build good credit from an early age can have lasting impacts on your financial well-being and open doors to future opportunities. Avoiding common credit mistakes is essential for maintaining a healthy credit profile and achieving long-term financial stability. Understanding these mistakes and knowing how to steer clear of them can help you build and maintain good credit, minimize interest costs, and safeguard your financial future.

Several key areas to focus on include timely payments, managing credit utilization, being cautious with new credit applications, and understanding the terms of your credit agreements. One of the most crucial aspects of maintaining good credit is ensuring that all payments are made on time. Late payments can have a significant negative impact on your credit score and can remain on your credit report for several years. Setting up automatic payments or reminders can help ensure that bills are paid by their due dates. It's also important to manage your cash flow effectively, so you have sufficient funds available to cover your payments. Even a single missed payment can damage your credit score, so consistently meeting payment deadlines is essential for maintaining a positive credit history. Another common credit mistake to avoid is high credit utilization. Credit utilization refers to the ratio of your credit card balances to your credit limits. High credit utilization can signal financial distress and negatively affect your credit score. To manage credit utilization effectively, aim to keep your credit card balances well below your credit limits. Ideally, you should strive to use less than 30% of your available credit. Paying off your credit card balances in full each month can help you maintain low credit utilization and avoid interest charges.

Be cautious with opening new credit accounts. Each time you apply for new credit, a hard inquiry is made on your credit report. Multiple hard inquiries within a short period can negatively impact your credit score, as they may suggest that you are seeking more credit than you can handle. Additionally, opening too many new credit accounts can shorten the average age of your credit history, which can also affect your credit score. It's important to apply for new credit only when necessary and to understand how each application might impact your credit profile. Understanding the terms and conditions of your credit agreements is another critical aspect of avoiding credit mistakes. Many people overlook the details of credit card agreements, loans, and other credit products, which can lead to unexpected fees or unfavorable terms. Carefully review the interest rates, fees, repayment schedules, and any penalties associated with your credit accounts. Knowing the specifics of your credit agreements can help you avoid surprises and make informed decisions about managing your credit.

Managing debt responsibly is also key to avoiding credit pitfalls. It's easy to accumulate debt if you're not careful about your spending and borrowing habits. Avoid taking on more debt than you can reasonably manage, and be mindful of your overall financial situation. Create a budget that includes your income, expenses, and debt payments to ensure you are living within your means. If you find yourself struggling with debt, consider seeking assistance from a financial advisor or credit counselor to develop a plan for managing and reducing your debt. Another common mistake is neglecting to monitor your credit reports regularly. Your credit report contains detailed information about your credit history, including accounts, payment history, and any negative marks. Regularly reviewing your credit reports allows you to check for accuracy, identify potential errors, and spot any signs of fraud or identity theft. You are entitled to receive a free credit report from each of the major credit bureaus—Equifax, Experian, and TransUnion—annually. By taking advantage of these free reports, you can stay informed about your credit status and address any issues promptly. Building and maintaining a good credit history requires patience and consistency. Avoid seeking instant credit solutions or making hasty financial decisions that could harm your credit profile. Establishing a positive credit history takes time and responsible financial behavior. Focus on making timely payments, managing credit utilization, and understanding your credit agreements to build a strong credit foundation.

It's also important to be cautious with credit-related promotions and offers. Many credit card companies and lenders offer enticing promotions, such as introductory 0% interest rates or rewards programs. While these offers can be beneficial, they often come with terms and conditions that may not be immediately apparent. Ensure you fully understand the fine print of any credit offers and consider whether the benefits outweigh any potential drawbacks. Avoid being swayed by promotional offers without thoroughly evaluating the terms and their impact on your credit. Avoiding common credit mistakes also involves maintaining a healthy balance between different types of credit. Having a mix of credit accounts, such as credit cards, installment loans, and retail accounts, can positively impact your credit score. However, it's important to manage each type of credit responsibly. Avoid opening unnecessary accounts simply to diversify your credit mix, as this can lead to additional inquiries and affect your credit score.

Finally, educating yourself about credit management and financial best practices can help you avoid common pitfalls. Stay informed about changes in credit reporting, interest rates, and financial products. Understanding how credit works and staying up-to-date with financial trends can empower you to make informed decisions and avoid mistakes that could negatively impact your credit. In conclusion, avoiding common credit mistakes involves a combination of timely payments, responsible credit utilization, cautious credit applications, and a thorough understanding of credit agreements. Regularly monitoring your credit reports, managing debt wisely, and being informed about credit-related offers can help you build and maintain a positive credit profile. By following these guidelines and practicing responsible credit management, you can safeguard your financial future and achieve long-term financial stability.

Understanding credit scores and how they affect your financial future is crucial for navigating the world of personal finance. A credit score is a numerical representation of your creditworthiness, which lenders use to assess the risk of lending you money. This score, typically ranging from 300 to 850, reflects your credit history and plays a significant role in determining the terms of credit and loan applications. Having a solid grasp of how credit scores work and their implications can help you make informed financial decisions and work towards a stable financial future. A credit score is calculated based on several key factors, each contributing to your overall credit profile. The most significant factors include your payment history, credit utilization, length of credit history, types of credit accounts, and recent credit inquiries. Payment history accounts for the largest portion of your credit score, reflecting your record of making timely payments on credit accounts. Consistently paying your bills on time is crucial for maintaining a positive credit score. Late payments, collections, or bankruptcies can have a substantial negative impact on your score.

Credit utilization, the ratio of your credit card balances to your credit limits, also plays a critical role in your credit score. High credit utilization can indicate financial distress and negatively affect your score. It is generally recommended to keep your credit utilization below 30% of your available credit to maintain a healthy score. By managing your credit card balances and keeping them low relative to your credit limits, you can contribute positively to your credit profile. The length of your credit history influences your score as well. A longer credit history provides more information about your credit behavior and demonstrates your experience in managing credit. Therefore, keeping old accounts open, even if you're not using them frequently, can benefit your credit score. Closing old accounts may shorten your credit history and potentially lower your score. However, it's also essential to manage your credit accounts responsibly to avoid any negative impacts.

The types of credit accounts you have, such as revolving credit cards, installment loans, and retail accounts, contribute to your credit score as well. Having a mix of different types of credit accounts shows lenders that you can manage various forms of credit responsibly. However, avoid taking on new credit accounts just to diversify your credit mix, as this can lead to unnecessary hard inquiries and affect your score. It's important to balance credit diversity with responsible management. Recent credit inquiries, or hard inquiries, occur when you apply for new credit. Each hard inquiry can have a small, temporary impact on your credit score. Multiple hard inquiries within a short period can signal that you are seeking excessive credit, which may lower your score. To minimize the impact of hard inquiries, apply for new credit only when necessary and be mindful of how each application affects your credit profile. Credit scores are classified into different ranges, each indicating varying levels of creditworthiness. Generally, scores are categorized as follows: excellent (750 and above), good (700 to 749), fair (650 to 699), and poor (below 650). A higher credit score reflects a lower risk to lenders and often results in better credit terms, such as lower interest rates on loans and credit cards. Conversely, a lower credit score may result in higher interest rates or difficulty obtaining credit.

The implications of your credit score extend beyond just borrowing costs. It affects various aspects of your financial life, including the ability to rent an apartment, secure a job, or obtain insurance. Landlords often use credit scores to screen potential tenants, and a higher score can improve your chances of securing a rental. Similarly, some employers check credit scores as part of their hiring process, particularly for positions involving financial responsibilities. Insurance companies may also consider your credit score when determining premiums, with higher scores potentially leading to lower rates. Maintaining a good credit score requires ongoing attention and management. Regularly monitoring your credit reports helps you stay informed about your credit status and identify any errors or discrepancies. You are entitled to receive a free credit report from each of the major credit bureaus—Equifax, Experian, and TransUnion—annually. Reviewing these reports allows you to ensure that the information is accurate and address any issues promptly.

Additionally, managing credit responsibly involves making timely payments, keeping credit utilization low, and avoiding excessive credit inquiries. Building and maintaining a positive credit history requires patience and consistent effort. By understanding how credit scores work and implementing strategies to improve and protect your score, you can enhance your financial well-being and secure better financial opportunities. In summary, understanding credit scores and their impact on your financial future is essential for making informed financial decisions. Your credit score reflects your creditworthiness and influences various aspects of your financial life, from loan terms to job prospects. By focusing on factors such as payment history, credit utilization, length of credit history, types of credit accounts, and recent credit inquiries, you can work towards maintaining a positive credit profile. Regularly monitoring your credit reports and practicing responsible credit management are key to achieving long-term financial stability and success.

Using credit cards responsibly is crucial for maintaining a healthy financial profile and avoiding debt-related issues. Credit cards, while offering convenience and benefits, can also lead to financial strain if not managed properly. Understanding how to use credit cards wisely involves several key practices, including timely payments, mindful spending, managing credit utilization, and understanding the terms of your credit card agreements. One of the fundamental principles of responsible credit card use is making timely payments. Credit card issuers report payment history to credit bureaus, and late payments can significantly impact your credit score. Setting up automatic payments or reminders can help ensure that you never miss a due date. Paying at least the minimum payment by the due date is essential, but paying off the full balance each month is even better. By avoiding interest charges and preventing debt accumulation, you can maintain a positive credit history and avoid unnecessary financial stress. Another critical aspect of responsible credit card use is managing your credit utilization. Credit utilization refers to the ratio of your credit card balances to your credit limits. High credit utilization can negatively affect your credit score and suggest financial instability. To maintain a healthy credit profile, aim to keep your credit card balances well below your credit limits. Ideally, your utilization should be under 30% of your available credit. Regularly reviewing your statements and adjusting your spending habits can help you stay within this recommended range.

Being mindful of your spending habits is also important for using credit cards responsibly. Credit cards can make it easy to overspend, especially if you are not keeping track of your purchases. Creating a budget that includes your credit card expenditures can help you stay on top of your spending and avoid accumulating debt. It's important to use credit cards for purchases that fit within your budget and to avoid impulsive buying. Keeping track of your credit card activity through mobile apps or online account management tools can provide real-time insights into your spending and help you make informed financial decisions. Understanding the terms and conditions of your credit card agreements is crucial for managing your credit card use effectively. Credit cards come with various terms, including interest rates, fees, rewards programs, and promotional offers. Familiarize yourself with the interest rates, including annual percentage rates (APRs) for purchases, balance transfers, and cash advances. Be aware of any fees associated with your card, such as annual fees, late payment fees, or foreign transaction fees. Understanding these terms helps you avoid unexpected charges and manage your credit card more effectively. Taking advantage of credit card rewards and benefits can be a positive aspect of responsible credit card use. Many credit cards offer rewards programs, cash back, travel benefits, or purchase protections. To maximize these benefits, choose a credit card that aligns with your spending habits and financial goals. For example, if you frequently travel, a card with travel rewards or perks might be beneficial. However, ensure that the rewards and benefits outweigh any associated costs or fees. It's also important to redeem rewards according to the card issuer's guidelines and make the most of the available perks.

Another important practice is to avoid accumulating unnecessary debt on your credit cards. While credit cards provide access to credit, it's essential to borrow responsibly and only for purchases you can afford to repay. Avoid using credit cards to cover regular expenses if you cannot pay off the balance in full each month. Accumulating debt can lead to high-interest charges and financial difficulties. If you find yourself struggling with credit card debt, consider developing a debt repayment plan or seeking advice from a financial counselor to help you manage and reduce your debt. Regularly monitoring your credit card statements is crucial for identifying any discrepancies or fraudulent activity. Review your statements each month to ensure that all charges are accurate and that no unauthorized transactions have occurred. Reporting any errors or suspicious activity promptly to your credit card issuer can help protect your account and minimize potential financial loss. Many credit card issuers offer online account management tools that make it easy to track and review your transactions.

Building a positive credit history with your credit card also involves maintaining a good credit card account balance. Avoid closing old credit card accounts, even if you are not using them frequently. The length of your credit history contributes to your credit score, and closing old accounts can shorten your credit history and potentially lower your score. Keeping old accounts open and managing them responsibly can benefit your credit profile over time. It's also important to be cautious with credit card applications and inquiries. Applying for multiple credit cards in a short period can result in several hard inquiries on your credit report, which can negatively impact your credit score. Each hard inquiry can suggest that you are seeking more credit than you can handle, potentially lowering your score. Apply for new credit cards only when necessary and be mindful of how each application might affect your credit profile.

Finally, educating yourself about credit card management and staying informed about financial best practices is essential for using credit cards responsibly. Understanding how credit cards work, including their benefits and potential pitfalls, empowers you to make informed decisions and avoid common mistakes. Stay updated on changes in credit card terms, interest rates, and financial regulations to ensure you are managing your credit cards effectively. Using credit cards responsibly involves making timely payments, managing credit utilization, being mindful of spending, and understanding the terms of your credit card agreements. By following these practices, you can maintain a positive credit history, avoid unnecessary debt, and make the most of your credit card benefits. Regular monitoring of your credit card statements and account balances, along with prudent credit card management, can contribute to long-term financial stability and success. Avoiding debt traps and learning to manage debt effectively are crucial for maintaining financial health and achieving long-term stability. Debt traps often arise from mismanagement, overspending, or taking on more debt than one can handle. Understanding how to avoid these pitfalls and implement strategies for managing debt can prevent financial difficulties and contribute to overall financial well-being.

One of the primary ways to avoid falling into debt traps is to live within your means. Creating a detailed budget that outlines your income, expenses, and savings goals is essential for staying on track financially. By tracking your spending and ensuring that it aligns with your income, you can prevent overspending and avoid accumulating debt. A well-structured budget helps you manage your finances more effectively, prioritize essential expenses, and allocate funds for savings and debt repayment.

Another key strategy for avoiding debt traps is to use credit responsibly. Credit cards and loans offer convenience but can lead to financial problems if not managed properly. Avoid using credit cards for purchases that you cannot afford to repay in full by the due date. Relying on credit cards for everyday expenses can quickly lead to high balances and accumulating interest charges. Instead, use credit cards for planned purchases and ensure that you pay off the balance in full each month to avoid interest and debt buildup. Managing existing debt is also crucial for avoiding debt traps. If you already have debt, it's important to develop a plan for repayment. Start by prioritizing high-interest debt, such as credit card balances, as it can accrue interest quickly and become more challenging to manage over time. Consider using the snowball or avalanche method for debt repayment. The snowball method involves paying off the smallest debt first while making minimum payments on larger debts, which can provide a psychological boost as debts are eliminated. The avalanche method focuses on paying off the debt with the highest interest rate first, which can save more money in the long run. Maintaining an emergency fund is another important aspect of avoiding debt traps. Unexpected expenses, such as medical bills or car repairs, can quickly lead to debt if you do not have sufficient savings set aside. Building an emergency fund helps you cover these unforeseen costs without relying on credit cards or loans. Aim to save three to six months' worth of living expenses in an easily accessible account to provide a financial cushion during times of need.

Understanding the terms and conditions of any debt you take on is crucial for managing it effectively. Before committing to a loan or credit card, review the interest rates, fees, and repayment terms. Be aware of any penalties for late payments, changes in interest rates, or fees associated with your debt. Fully understanding these terms helps you make informed decisions and avoid unexpected financial burdens. If you have questions about your debt agreements, don't hesitate to reach out to your lender or financial advisor for clarification. Avoiding unnecessary debt is another important aspect of financial management. Resist the temptation to take on new debt for non-essential purchases or lifestyle upgrades. Before applying for new credit or loans, evaluate whether the debt is necessary and if you can realistically afford the repayments. Consider saving for large purchases instead of using credit to finance them. Responsible borrowing and spending practices contribute to long-term financial health and prevent debt traps.

It's also important to be proactive in managing and monitoring your credit. Regularly review your credit reports to ensure that all information is accurate and up-to-date. Discrepancies or errors on your credit report can impact your credit score and affect your ability to manage debt effectively. You are entitled to receive a free credit report from each of the major credit bureaus—Equifax, Experian, and TransUnion—annually. Monitoring your credit reports helps you stay informed about your credit status and address any issues promptly. If you find yourself struggling with debt, seeking professional help can be beneficial. Credit counseling services offer guidance on managing debt, creating budgets, and developing debt repayment plans. Financial advisors or credit counselors can work with you to create a personalized strategy for managing and reducing your debt. They can also provide valuable insights into negotiating with creditors or exploring debt consolidation options if needed.

Another effective strategy for managing debt is to consider debt consolidation. Debt consolidation involves combining multiple debts into a single loan or credit card with a lower interest rate. This can simplify debt management by reducing the number of payments you need to make and potentially lowering your overall interest costs. However, it's important to carefully evaluate the terms of any consolidation loan or balance transfer offer to ensure that it is beneficial and does not lead to additional debt. Avoiding debt traps also involves being mindful of your financial behavior and making conscious decisions about spending and borrowing. Developing good financial habits, such as setting financial goals, tracking expenses, and practicing disciplined spending, can help you stay on top of your finances and avoid falling into debt traps.

Regularly reviewing your budget and adjusting it as needed ensures that you remain aligned with your financial goals and can manage your debt effectively. Avoiding debt traps and learning to manage debt involves a combination of proactive financial planning and responsible credit use. By living within your means, managing existing debt, maintaining an emergency fund, understanding debt terms, and avoiding unnecessary debt, you can prevent financial difficulties and work towards long-term financial stability. Regularly monitoring your credit, seeking professional help when needed, and practicing good financial habits contribute to effective debt management and overall financial health. Exploring case studies of teens using credit responsibly provides valuable insights into how young individuals can successfully manage credit and build a strong financial foundation. These real-life examples illustrate different approaches to responsible credit use and the positive impact it can have on financial well-being. By examining these cases, teens can gain practical knowledge and inspiration for their own financial journeys.

One compelling case is that of Emma, a high school senior who began using a credit card responsibly at the age of 18. Emma's parents encouraged her to apply for a credit card to start building her credit history, but they also provided guidance on how to use it wisely. Emma was given a credit card with a low limit to ensure she wouldn't overspend. She made a habit of using her card only for planned purchases, such as buying textbooks or paying for monthly subscriptions. Emma set up automatic payments to ensure her credit card bill was paid in full each month, avoiding interest charges and late fees. Emma also tracked her spending using a budgeting app, which helped her stay within her limits and manage her finances effectively. She made it a priority to keep her credit utilization below 30% of her credit limit, ensuring that she was not overextending herself. Emma's responsible use of credit contributed to a positive credit history, which helped her secure a favorable interest rate on a car loan after graduation. Her early experiences with credit taught her valuable lessons about financial discipline and the importance of maintaining a good credit score.

Another notable case is that of Liam, a college student who managed his credit card with a strategic approach to debt management. Liam used his credit card for essential expenses and emergencies, but he was cautious about taking on unnecessary debt. To avoid accumulating high-interest debt, Liam paid off his balance in full each month and kept track of his spending through a detailed budget. When Liam received a credit card offer with a low introductory interest rate, he carefully reviewed the terms before accepting it, ensuring that he understood the long-term implications. Liam's approach to credit card use included setting aside a portion of his monthly income for debt repayment and savings. He maintained a small credit card balance to build credit but avoided carrying a high balance that could lead to financial strain. By staying disciplined with his credit use and focusing on his budget, Liam successfully managed his credit card without falling into debt traps. His responsible credit use allowed him to build a strong credit history, which was beneficial when he applied for student loans and rental agreements.

Another example is Sarah, a teen who used her credit card to develop a healthy credit history and achieve financial goals. Sarah's parents taught her the importance of responsible credit use from an early age and encouraged her to start with a credit card that offered rewards for everyday purchases. Sarah used her credit card to buy groceries, pay for transportation, and cover other routine expenses. She carefully managed her spending to ensure that she did not exceed her budget and made a habit of paying off her credit card balance in full each month. Sarah also took advantage of financial education resources and attended workshops on credit management. These resources helped her understand the nuances of credit scores, interest rates, and credit utilization. As a result, Sarah was well-informed about her credit card terms and made informed decisions about her credit use. Her proactive approach to financial education and responsible credit management enabled her to build a strong credit profile, which proved advantageous when she needed to secure a loan for a study abroad program. A final example is Alex, a young entrepreneur who used credit responsibly to support his small business. At 19, Alex started an online business selling handmade crafts and needed a credit card to manage business expenses and cash flow. He used his credit card to purchase supplies and cover marketing costs, but he was diligent about paying off the balance each month to avoid interest charges. Alex kept detailed records of his business expenses and income, which allowed him to track his financial performance and ensure he was not overspending.

Alex also set up a separate savings account for his business to build an emergency fund and manage unexpected expenses. By maintaining a clear separation between personal and business finances, Alex was able to manage his credit card use effectively and maintain a healthy credit profile. His responsible credit practices and financial management skills contributed to the success of his business and helped him build a positive credit history. These case studies demonstrate that teens can use credit responsibly by adopting sound financial practices and making informed decisions. Key strategies for responsible credit use include making timely payments, managing credit utilization, tracking spending, and understanding credit card terms. Each of these examples highlights the importance of financial discipline, budgeting, and proactive credit management in building a strong credit history and achieving financial goals.

By following these examples and applying similar principles, teens can set themselves up for long-term financial success and avoid common pitfalls associated with credit use.

1. Assess Your Current Credit Situation:

Obtain a copy of your credit report from each of the major credit bureaus: Equifax, Experian, and TransUnion. You are entitled to one free report per year from each bureau.

- Date you will request your reports: _____

- Review your credit reports for accuracy. Check for any errors or discrepancies.

- Describe any errors or discrepancies you find: _____

- Note your current credit score and understand what factors are influencing it.

- Your current credit score: _____

- Factors influencing your credit score: _____

2. Set Clear Credit Goals:

- Define what you want to achieve with your credit. Examples might include qualifying for a credit card, securing a loan, or obtaining a lower interest rate.

- Your credit goals:

  _____

- Set short-term and long-term goals.

- Short-term goal (e.g., increase score by 50 points in 6 months):

  _____

- Long-term goal (e.g., maintain an excellent credit score):

  _____

3. Create a Budget:

- Develop a monthly budget that includes income, expenses, and savings goals. Ensure funds are allocated for debt repayment and other financial obligations.

- Monthly budget plan: _____

- Track your spending and adjust your budget as needed.

- How you will track spending: _____

4. Establish a Credit-Building Strategy:

- Open a credit account. Consider applying for a secured credit card or a beginner's credit card if you have little or no credit history.

- Type of credit account you will open: _____

- Use credit responsibly. Charge only what you can afford to pay off each month.

- How much you plan to charge each month: _____

- Make timely payments. Set up automatic payments or reminders.

- Payment reminders or automatic payment setup: _____

5. Manage Your Credit Utilization:

- Aim to use less than 30% of your available credit limit.

- Current credit limit: _____

- Target balance (30% of limit): _____

- Monitor your credit card balances regularly.

- Frequency of monitoring: _____

6. Monitor Your Credit Reports:

- Regularly review your credit reports to track progress and identify issues.

- How often you will review your reports: _____

- Dispute inaccuracies or fraudulent accounts.

- Steps for disputing inaccuracies: _____

7. Avoid Common Credit Mistakes:

- Don't apply for too much credit. Apply only when necessary.

- How you will limit credit applications: _____

- Avoid closing old accounts.

- Decision on keeping old accounts: _____

8. Build a Positive Credit History:

- Diversify your credit if it suits your financial situation.

- Types of credit accounts you plan to have: _____

- Maintain an emergency fund.

- Emergency fund goal: _____

9. Evaluate and Adjust Your Plan:

- Periodically review your credit-building plan.

- When you will review your plan: _____

- Set new goals or strategies as needed.

- New goals or strategies: _____

10. Seek Professional Advice:

- If you face difficulties or have questions, consult a financial advisor or credit counselor.

- Contact information for professional advice: _____

By completing these sections, you will have a personalized plan to build and maintain good credit. Responsible credit use and careful financial management are key to achieving your credit goals and ensuring long-term stability.

CHAPTER 8

EARNING MONEY: JOBS, SIDE HUSTLES, AND ENTREPRENEURSHIP

Earning money as a teen is an essential aspect of financial independence and personal growth. It provides valuable experience, teaches responsibility, and helps develop skills that will be beneficial throughout life. For teenagers, there are a variety of ways to generate income, each with its unique set of opportunities and challenges. From traditional part-time jobs to modern freelance work and entrepreneurial ventures, exploring these options can help teens find the best fit for their interests and goals. Part-time jobs are often the first step for many teens looking to earn money. These jobs typically offer a regular schedule and a steady income, providing a solid foundation for financial management. Common part-time positions include roles in retail, food service, and customer support. Working at a local store or restaurant can teach valuable lessons in time management, customer service, and teamwork.

Additionally, these jobs can provide a structured work environment, where teens learn to balance work responsibilities with school and personal life. Part-time jobs can also serve as a stepping stone to more advanced career opportunities, offering experiences that are attractive to future employers. Freelance work represents another growing opportunity for teens to earn money. The rise of digital platforms has made it easier than ever for individuals to offer their skills and services to a global market. Freelancing allows teens to leverage their talents in areas such as writing, graphic design, programming, or social media management. Platforms like Upwork, Fiverr, and Freelancer provide a marketplace where teens can connect with clients seeking their expertise. Freelancing offers flexibility in terms of work hours and project selection, making it an attractive option for those with busy schedules or specific interests. It also helps teens build a professional portfolio and gain experience in managing client relationships and meeting deadlines. Side hustles have become increasingly popular among teens seeking to supplement their income or explore entrepreneurial interests. Unlike traditional jobs, side hustles often involve a more creative or independent approach to earning money. Examples of side hustles include starting a blog, selling handmade crafts online, or offering tutoring services. These ventures allow teens to explore their passions and turn hobbies into income-generating activities. Side hustles can be a way to test entrepreneurial ideas and build a business from the ground up. They also provide opportunities to learn about marketing, finance, and business management, skills that are valuable in any career.

Entrepreneurship offers another avenue for teens to earn money while developing leadership and business skills. Starting a business, whether it's a small online shop, a service-based company, or a local venture, requires creativity, initiative, and a willingness to take risks. Entrepreneurs must handle various aspects of running a business, including product development, marketing, and customer service. For teens interested in entrepreneurship, there are numerous resources available, such as online courses, mentorship programs, and community business incubators. Entrepreneurship fosters a sense of independence and self-reliance, teaching teens how to navigate challenges and seize opportunities. Each of these earning methods has its benefits and considerations. Part-time jobs provide stability and a structured work environment but may offer limited flexibility. Freelance work offers independence and a range of projects but requires self-discipline and the ability to manage multiple clients. Side hustles and entrepreneurial ventures offer creative freedom and the potential for significant growth but come with the challenges of starting and managing a business. Understanding the different options and evaluating personal interests and goals can help teens make informed decisions about how to earn money. In addition to earning money, these opportunities also offer valuable life lessons. Working part-time helps develop a strong work ethic and interpersonal skills, while freelancing and side hustles teach self-management and entrepreneurial thinking. Entrepreneurship, in particular, encourages problem-solving, innovation, and perseverance. Each experience contributes to personal development and prepares teens for future careers and financial responsibilities. As teens explore ways to earn money, it's important to consider legal and practical aspects, such as labor laws, tax implications, and time management. Understanding these factors ensures that teens are well-prepared and compliant with regulations while pursuing their earning goals. Seeking guidance from parents, mentors, or career counselors can provide additional support and insights. Earning money as a teen encompasses a range of opportunities, from part-time jobs to freelance work, side hustles, and entrepreneurship. Each option offers unique benefits and challenges, allowing teens to choose the path that best aligns with their interests, skills, and goals. By exploring these various methods, teens can gain valuable experience, develop essential skills, and take significant steps toward financial independence and personal growth.

Finding work that fits both your schedule and interests is crucial for maintaining motivation and ensuring a positive work experience. Balancing personal preferences with practical considerations can make a significant difference in job satisfaction and overall performance. Here are several tips to help you find work that aligns with your schedule and interests, enabling you to manage your time effectively while pursuing opportunities that you are passionate about. Start by identifying your interests and strengths. Understanding what you enjoy and where your talents lie can help you target opportunities that are both fulfilling and suited to your skills. Take time to reflect on your hobbies, subjects you excel in, or activities that bring you joy. This self-assessment will guide you in choosing roles that align with your passions, making the work more enjoyable and engaging. For instance, if you have a knack for writing, you might consider freelance writing or content creation. If you are passionate about art, opportunities in graphic design or illustration might be ideal. Next, consider your schedule and time commitments. Balancing work with school, extracurricular activities, or family responsibilities requires careful planning. Determine how many hours a week you can realistically dedicate to a job and what times of day you are available. Some positions, such as part-time retail jobs, may offer fixed shifts that align with your availability, while freelance work or side hustles might provide more flexibility. Be clear about your time constraints when applying for jobs or negotiating work hours to ensure that you can manage your responsibilities effectively. Look for job opportunities that offer flexible schedules. Many positions, especially in the gig economy, provide flexibility that allows you to choose when and how much you work. Freelancing, for example, often allows you to set your own hours and work from anywhere. Similarly, remote internships or virtual assistant roles can offer flexibility that fits around your existing commitments. Online job boards and platforms like Upwork, Fiverr, and FlexJobs can help you find opportunities with flexible scheduling options.

Utilize your network to find job opportunities that match your interests and schedule. Reach out to family, friends, teachers, or mentors who might know of openings that fit your criteria. Networking can provide valuable insights and connections that are not always advertised publicly. Informing people within your network about your job search can lead to recommendations and opportunities that you might not have discovered on your own. Additionally, attending career fairs or industry events can expose you to potential employers who are seeking candidates with specific interests and availability. Research potential employers to understand their work culture and flexibility. Before applying for a job, gather information about the company's work environment and policies. Look for reviews from current or former employees, which can provide insights into how accommodating the employer is regarding work schedules. Some companies may offer flexible hours, remote work options, or part-time positions that cater to varying needs. Understanding these aspects can help you determine whether a job aligns with both your personal interests and scheduling requirements. Consider part-time and temporary positions as viable options. These types of roles can offer the flexibility to work around your existing commitments while gaining valuable experience. Part-time jobs, such as working at a local store or café, often provide a set number of hours per week, allowing you to balance work with other activities. Temporary positions or seasonal work can also offer short-term opportunities that fit specific time frames, such as summer internships or holiday retail jobs. These roles can help you build experience and earn income without a long-term commitment. Explore opportunities for remote or virtual work. With the rise of technology and digital communication, many jobs can now be performed remotely, offering greater flexibility in terms of location and hours. Remote work options might include roles such as virtual assistants, online tutors, or freelance writers. These positions often allow you to work from home or any location with an internet connection, giving you more control over your schedule and work environment. Research remote job boards or websites that specialize in virtual work to find opportunities that suit your needs.

Be open to internships or volunteer work that aligns with your interests. While these roles may not always provide immediate financial compensation, they offer valuable experience and networking opportunities that can benefit your future career. Internships and volunteer positions can help you gain skills, build a professional network, and explore your interests in a practical setting. They can also lead to paid opportunities or job offers down the line. Look for internships or volunteer opportunities in fields related to your passions to gain relevant experience and make meaningful connections. Finally, be proactive in managing your job search and application process. Tailor your resume and cover letter to highlight your skills, interests, and availability. When applying for jobs, clearly communicate your schedule constraints and preferences to potential employers. Being upfront about your needs ensures that you are considered for positions that align with your requirements. Additionally, follow up on applications and interviews to demonstrate your enthusiasm and commitment to finding the right fit. Finding work that fits your schedule and interests involves a combination of self-assessment, research, and proactive job searching. By understanding your interests, considering your time commitments, and exploring various job options, you can identify opportunities that align with your personal and professional goals. Utilizing your network, researching potential employers, and being open to flexible or remote roles can further enhance your chances of finding a job that is both rewarding and manageable. Through careful planning and consideration, you can achieve a balance that supports your growth and success in the workforce.

Balancing work, school, and social life is a common challenge for teenagers striving to juggle multiple responsibilities while maintaining their well-being. Successfully managing these different aspects of life requires careful planning, organization, and self-awareness. By implementing effective strategies, teens can achieve a harmonious balance that allows them to excel academically, perform well in their jobs, and enjoy their social lives. One of the foundational steps to achieving balance is effective time management. Creating a detailed schedule that includes all your commitments—such as school, work, extracurricular activities, and social events—can help you visualize how your time is allocated. Use a planner, calendar, or digital app to map out your daily, weekly, and monthly activities. This approach allows you to identify potential conflicts and ensure that you have adequate time for each of your responsibilities. By prioritizing tasks and setting clear deadlines, you can manage your time more efficiently and reduce the risk of becoming overwhelmed. Setting realistic goals and expectations is also crucial for maintaining balance. It's important to understand your limits and avoid overcommitting yourself. Assess your workload and personal commitments to determine what is achievable within a given timeframe. Set specific, manageable goals for your schoolwork, job performance, and social activities. Break larger tasks into smaller, more manageable steps to make them less daunting and more attainable. By setting realistic goals, you can ensure that you are not stretching yourself too thin and can focus on completing tasks effectively.

Developing a routine can provide structure and stability in your daily life. Establishing consistent study times, work hours, and social activities helps create a sense of predictability and order. A well-defined routine can also help you build productive habits and reduce stress. For example, setting aside specific times each day for studying and completing assignments can help you stay on top of your academic responsibilities. Similarly, scheduling regular breaks and leisure activities ensures that you have time to relax and recharge. Effective communication with employers, teachers, and friends is essential for balancing work, school, and social life. Be open and honest about your commitments and schedule constraints with your employer, especially if you need flexibility with your work hours. Inform your teachers about any potential conflicts with assignments or exams due to work commitments. Communication helps build understanding and allows you to negotiate adjustments when necessary. Additionally, keep your friends informed about your schedule and availability, so they understand when you may be unable to participate in social activities. Learning to manage stress and maintain your well-being is crucial for achieving balance. High levels of stress can negatively impact your performance in school, at work, and in social settings. Incorporate stress-relief techniques into your routine, such as exercise, meditation, or hobbies that you enjoy. Prioritize self-care by ensuring you get enough sleep, eat a balanced diet, and take time for relaxation. Recognize signs of burnout and take proactive steps to address them, such as taking breaks or seeking support from a counselor or mentor.

Being organized and staying on top of deadlines can significantly ease the pressure of balancing multiple responsibilities. Use organizational tools like to-do lists, reminder apps, or task management software to keep track of assignments, work shifts, and social events. Plan ahead for upcoming deadlines and obligations to avoid last-minute stress. Regularly review your schedule and adjust as needed to accommodate any changes or unexpected events. Finding ways to integrate your activities can also help streamline your schedule. For example, if you have a long commute to work or school, use that time to listen to educational podcasts or audiobooks related to your studies. Combine social activities with other commitments, such as inviting friends to join you for a study session or exercising together. By integrating activities, you can maximize your time and make the most of your commitments. Building a support network is another important aspect of maintaining balance. Surround yourself with supportive friends, family members, and mentors who understand your goals and can offer encouragement and advice. Share your challenges and successes with your support network, and seek their input on how to manage your responsibilities effectively. A strong support system can provide emotional support and practical solutions for balancing work, school, and social life.

Additionally, be flexible and willing to adjust your plans as needed. Life is unpredictable, and there may be times when unexpected events or changes in priorities require you to reassess your schedule. Be prepared to adapt and make necessary adjustments to maintain balance. Flexibility allows you to navigate challenges more effectively and ensures that you can respond to changing circumstances without becoming overwhelmed. Lastly, regularly evaluate your balance and make adjustments as necessary. Periodically review your schedule, commitments, and stress levels to assess whether your current approach is working. Reflect on what is going well and identify areas where improvements can be made. Adjust your goals, routines, and priorities based on your evaluation to continue maintaining a healthy balance. In summary, balancing work, school, and social life requires effective time management, realistic goal setting, and a well-structured routine. Effective communication, stress management, and organizational skills also play a key role in achieving balance. By integrating activities, building a support network, and remaining flexible, teens can navigate their various responsibilities successfully while maintaining their well-being. Regularly evaluating and adjusting your approach ensures that you continue to manage your commitments effectively and enjoy a fulfilling and balanced life.

Starting a small business or side hustle involves a series of essential steps and considerations that can set the foundation for success. To begin with, it is important to identify a viable business idea or side hustle that aligns with your interests, skills, and market demand. Conducting thorough research is crucial to understanding the needs and preferences of your target audience, as well as assessing potential competition. This research helps in shaping your business concept and ensuring that there is a demand for the product or service you intend to offer. Once you have a clear idea, the next step is to develop a solid business plan. A business plan outlines your goals, strategies, target market, and financial projections. It serves as a roadmap for your business and is essential for securing funding if needed. Your business plan should include an analysis of your competition, a marketing strategy to attract customers, and a financial plan detailing your startup costs, expected revenue, and budgeting. This plan not only helps in organizing your thoughts and strategies but also provides a framework for measuring progress and making adjustments as needed. Securing funding is another critical step in starting a business or side hustle. Depending on the scale of your venture, you might need to explore different financing options such as personal savings, loans, or investments. For a small side hustle, initial costs might be minimal, but for a larger business, you may need to seek external funding from investors or financial institutions. It is important to understand the terms and conditions associated with any funding you pursue and ensure that you have a clear plan for managing and repaying any borrowed funds. Setting up the legal structure of your business is also essential. This includes choosing a business name, registering it with the appropriate government authorities, and obtaining any necessary licenses or permits. The legal structure you choose, such as sole proprietorship, partnership, LLC, or corporation, will impact your liability, taxes, and administrative requirements. It's important to research and select the structure that best suits your business needs and consult with legal or financial professionals if needed.

Developing a brand and marketing strategy is crucial for attracting and retaining customers. Your brand encompasses your business name, logo, and overall identity, which should reflect the values and image you want to project. Create a marketing plan that outlines how you will reach your target audience through various channels such as social media, email marketing, or local advertising. Building an online presence through a website or social media platforms can also enhance your visibility and help in connecting with potential customers. Once your business is up and running, focus on providing excellent customer service and building relationships with your clients. Positive customer experiences can lead to repeat business and referrals, which are vital for growth. Monitor customer feedback and be open to making improvements based on their suggestions. Additionally, keep track of your finances by maintaining accurate records of your income and expenses. Regularly reviewing your financial statements helps in managing cash flow, budgeting effectively, and ensuring profitability. Scaling your business or side hustle involves planning for growth and expansion. As your business gains traction, you may consider increasing your product or service offerings, expanding to new markets, or hiring additional staff. Effective scaling requires careful planning and analysis to ensure that growth is sustainable and manageable. Continuously evaluate your business performance and adapt your strategies to meet evolving market demands.

Throughout the process of starting and running a business or side hustle, it is important to stay motivated and resilient. Challenges and setbacks are a natural part of the entrepreneurial journey. Maintaining a positive attitude, seeking support from mentors or peers, and being adaptable in the face of obstacles can contribute to long-term success. In summary, starting a small business or side hustle involves identifying a viable idea, developing a comprehensive business plan, securing funding, setting up the legal structure, and creating a brand and marketing strategy. Providing excellent customer service and managing finances effectively are key to running a successful venture. As your business grows, scaling strategically and staying motivated are essential for achieving long-term success. By following these foundational steps, you can set the stage for a successful entrepreneurial endeavor and turn your business ideas into reality.

Turning hobbies into income is an inspiring way for teens to blend their passions with financial opportunities. Through creativity and dedication, several teenagers have transformed their hobbies into successful income-generating ventures. These case studies illustrate how personal interests can evolve into profitable businesses, demonstrating the potential for turning passions into real-world success.

One notable example is Emma, a 17-year-old high school student who turned her love for baking into a thriving small business. Emma had always enjoyed baking for her friends and family, experimenting with new recipes and techniques. Recognizing the potential for her hobby to generate income, she decided to start a small baking business from her home kitchen. Emma began by offering custom cakes and cupcakes for local events and celebrations. She leveraged social media platforms to showcase her creations and attract clients. By consistently delivering high-quality products and excellent customer service, Emma quickly gained a loyal customer base. Her business grew through word-of-mouth referrals, and she even started offering baking classes for children. Emma's story highlights how a passion for baking, combined with effective marketing and customer engagement, can lead to a successful income-generating venture.

Another inspiring case is that of Jake, a 16-year-old with a keen interest in video gaming. Jake was an avid gamer and had a natural talent for creating engaging content related to video games. He decided to turn this hobby into a side hustle by starting a YouTube channel dedicated to gaming tutorials, reviews, and live streaming. Initially, Jake invested in basic recording equipment and spent time learning about video editing and content creation. As he consistently produced high-quality videos and interacted with his audience, his channel began to gain traction. Through ad revenue, sponsorships, and merchandise sales, Jake was able to generate a steady stream of income from his channel. His success demonstrates how a passion for gaming and content creation, coupled with perseverance and creativity, can lead to a profitable online business.

In another example, Ava, a 15-year-old with a flair for arts and crafts, turned her hobby into a successful online store. Ava had always enjoyed creating handmade jewelry, painting, and crafting unique items. She decided to start an online shop where she could sell her handmade creations. Ava used platforms like Etsy to set up her store and showcased her products through social media channels. She focused on creating high-quality, unique items that appealed to her target audience. Ava's dedication to her craft and effective use of online platforms allowed her to reach a global customer base. Her business not only provided her with additional income but also helped her develop valuable skills in marketing, customer service, and inventory management.

Additionally, Ryan, a 17-year-old with a passion for photography, transformed his hobby into a profitable side hustle. Ryan had always enjoyed taking photos and experimenting with different styles. Recognizing the growing demand for high-quality images for social media and online content, he began offering his photography services to local businesses and individuals. Ryan created a portfolio showcasing his best work and used social media to promote his services. He also offered photography workshops and tutorials to share his knowledge with others. Through consistent networking and high-quality work, Ryan built a strong client base and developed a reputation as a talented photographer. His journey illustrates how a passion for photography, combined with business acumen and networking skills, can lead to a successful income-generating venture.

Another compelling case is that of Mia, a 16-year-old with a talent for writing. Mia enjoyed writing short stories, poems, and articles in her free time. She decided to explore ways to monetize her writing skills by starting a blog and offering freelance writing services. Mia focused on creating content that resonated with her audience and actively sought opportunities to contribute to various online publications. Her writing gained attention and she was able to secure paid writing gigs, including content creation for websites and promotional materials for local businesses. Mia's success demonstrates how a passion for writing, coupled with persistence and networking, can lead to a rewarding and profitable career.

These case studies highlight the diverse ways in which teens can turn their hobbies into income. Whether through baking, gaming, crafting, photography, or writing, each example demonstrates the potential for transforming personal interests into successful ventures. Key factors in their success include identifying a niche market, leveraging online platforms, maintaining high standards of quality, and engaging with their target audience. By following their examples and applying similar principles, other teens can explore opportunities to turn their hobbies into profitable endeavors, achieving both personal fulfillment and financial independence.

Brainstorm Ways to Earn Money and Develop a Plan

1. Identify Your Interests and Skills:

Start by listing your hobbies, passions, and skills. Consider what activities you enjoy and what you are good at. This could include anything from graphic design and writing to cooking or coding. Your interests and skills will help you identify potential ways to earn money.

List your hobbies, passions, and skills:

---

2. Explore Different Income Streams:

Based on your list of interests and skills, brainstorm various ways to monetize them. Think about both traditional and modern avenues. For example:

- Part-time Jobs: Retail, food service, tutoring.

- Freelance Work: Writing, graphic design, web development.

- Side Hustles: Selling handmade crafts online, offering pet sitting services, or running a blog.

- Entrepreneurial Ventures: Starting a small business, creating an online store, or launching a YouTube channel.

Your potential income streams:

---

3. Research Market Demand:

For each idea, conduct brief research to understand the demand in your area or online. Look at potential competitors, target audiences, and market trends. Use online tools, such as Google Trends or social media platforms, to gauge interest and identify gaps in the market.

Market demand for your ideas:

---

4. Evaluate Feasibility:

Assess the feasibility of each idea. Consider factors such as startup costs, time commitment, required skills, and potential income. Determine if you have the resources and capability to pursue each option.

Feasibility assessment for each idea:

---

5. Select Your Top Ideas:

Based on your research and evaluation, choose a few of the most promising ideas that align with your interests and have good market potential. Focus on ideas that are both feasible and exciting to you.

Your top ideas:

---

6. Develop a Plan:

For each selected idea, create a detailed plan that includes the following components:

Goals: Define what you want to achieve with your chosen idea. Set specific, measurable, attainable, relevant, and time-bound (SMART) goals.

Goals for your idea:

_____

Target Audience: Identify who your potential customers are and how you will reach them. Consider their needs, preferences, and how your offering will benefit them.

Target audience:

_____

Marketing Strategy: Outline how you will promote your idea. This could include social media marketing, word-of-mouth, or local advertising. Plan how you will create awareness and attract customers.

Marketing strategy:

_____

Budget: Estimate your startup costs and ongoing expenses. Determine how much you need to invest and how you will manage your finances. Include costs for materials, marketing, and any other necessary expenses.

Budget:

_____

Timeline: Set a timeline for launching your idea and achieving your goals. Create a schedule with milestones to track your progress and stay on track.

Timeline and milestones:

_____

7. Create an Action Plan:

Break down your plan into actionable steps. List the specific tasks you need to complete to get started. This might include setting up a website, designing marketing materials, or reaching out to potential customers. Assign deadlines to each task to ensure you stay organized and motivated.

Actionable steps and deadlines:

---

8. Seek Feedback:

Share your plan with trusted friends, family, or mentors to get their feedback. They can provide valuable insights, suggest improvements, and help you refine your approach.

Feedback received:

---

9. Take Action:

Begin implementing your plan by starting with the first few steps. Monitor your progress, adjust your plan as needed, and stay committed to your goals.

Initial steps taken:

---

10. Reflect and Adapt:

Periodically review your progress and reflect on what's working and what isn't. Be open to making adjustments based on feedback and changes in the market. Adapt your approach as needed to improve your chances of success.

Reflections and adjustments:

By completing these sections, you will have a structured approach to brainstorming ways to earn money and developing a plan to turn your ideas into action.

Chapter 9

SETTING FINANCIAL GOALS: HOW TO PLAN FOR THE FUTURE

Setting financial goals is a crucial step in achieving financial stability, security, and ultimately, freedom. It provides a roadmap for your financial journey, giving you direction and purpose in your money management efforts. Without clear financial goals, it's easy to fall into a pattern of aimless spending and saving, never quite sure if you're making progress or just treading water. Financial goals act as a compass, guiding your financial decisions and helping you prioritize where to allocate your resources. One of the primary reasons setting financial goals is essential is that it helps you focus on what's truly important to you. In a world filled with endless consumption opportunities and financial products, it's easy to get distracted and lose sight of what you really want to achieve with your money. By taking the time to define your financial goals, you're forced to reflect on your values, aspirations, and what you want your future to look like. This process of self-reflection can be incredibly valuable, not just for your finances but for your overall life direction. Financial goals also provide motivation and a sense of purpose to your financial activities. Saving money for the sake of saving can feel abstract and unrewarding. However, when you're saving for a specific goal, such as a down payment on a house, a dream vacation, or a comfortable retirement, it becomes much more tangible and exciting. This concrete vision of what you're working towards can be a powerful motivator, helping you stay committed to your savings plan even when temptations to spend arise.

Moreover, having clear financial goals allows you to measure your progress. Without specific targets, it's difficult to know if you're moving in the right direction or if your financial efforts are paying off. Goals provide benchmarks against which you can assess your financial health and progress. This ability to track your advancement is not only practically useful but can also be psychologically rewarding. Seeing yourself get closer to your goals can provide a sense of accomplishment and encourage you to keep pushing forward. Setting financial goals also helps in prioritizing your spending and saving decisions. In a world of limited resources, we constantly face trade-offs in how we use our money. Having clear goals makes it easier to decide where to allocate your funds. When faced with a spending decision, you can ask yourself whether it aligns with your financial goals. This framework can help you make more intentional choices about your money, reducing impulsive spending and ensuring that your financial resources are directed towards what truly matters to you. Financial goals are essential for both short-term financial management and long-term financial planning. In the short term, goals can help you manage your day-to-day finances more effectively. For example, setting a goal to build an emergency fund can motivate you to set aside a portion of each paycheck, ensuring you have a financial cushion for unexpected expenses. In the long term, goals like saving for retirement or paying off a mortgage provide a framework for making significant financial decisions that will impact your life for years to come.

Another crucial aspect of setting financial goals is that it encourages you to think about the future. In our daily lives, it's easy to get caught up in immediate concerns and short-term thinking. Financial goals force you to look ahead and consider your future needs and wants. This forward-thinking mindset is crucial for financial success, as many important financial decisions, such as saving for retirement or investing for long-term growth, require a long-term perspective. Setting financial goals also helps in developing a more comprehensive understanding of your financial situation. The process of setting goals often involves assessing your current financial state, including your income, expenses, assets, and liabilities. This comprehensive review can provide valuable insights into your financial health and areas that may need improvement. It can highlight gaps in your financial plan, such as inadequate insurance coverage or the need for estate planning, which you might otherwise overlook. Financial goals are also essential for couples and families to align their financial priorities. Money can be a significant source of conflict in relationships, often due to differing values and priorities when it comes to spending and saving. By setting financial goals together, couples can have open discussions about their financial aspirations and work towards common objectives. This shared vision can strengthen relationships and reduce financial stress. Moreover, having clear financial goals can provide a sense of control and reduce anxiety about money. Financial stress is a common issue for many people, often stemming from feelings of uncertainty or lack of control over their financial situation. By setting goals and working towards them, you create a sense of direction and purpose in your financial life. This can help alleviate anxiety and give you confidence in your ability to manage your finances effectively.

Financial goals also play a crucial role in risk management. Different financial goals often require different levels of risk tolerance. For example, short-term goals like saving for a vacation might be best served by low-risk, highly liquid savings accounts. In contrast, long-term goals like retirement savings might allow for higher-risk, potentially higher-return investments. By clearly defining your goals, you can better assess the appropriate level of risk for each financial objective and allocate your assets accordingly. Setting financial goals is also important because it encourages regular review and adjustment of your financial plan. As life circumstances change, so too might your financial goals. Regular goal-setting and review sessions prompt you to reassess your objectives and ensure they still align with your current situation and future aspirations. This ongoing process of evaluation and adjustment is crucial for maintaining a relevant and effective financial strategy throughout the various stages of your life.

Furthermore, financial goals can serve as a powerful tool for education and skill development. In the process of working towards your goals, you're likely to learn more about various financial concepts, investment strategies, and money management techniques. This increased financial literacy can be beneficial not just for achieving your current goals but for making informed financial decisions throughout your life. It's also worth noting that setting financial goals can have positive spillover effects into other areas of your life. The discipline and planning skills you develop in pursuing your financial objectives can be applied to other aspects of your life, such as career planning or personal development. The sense of accomplishment from achieving financial goals can boost your overall confidence and self-efficacy. While the importance of setting financial goals is clear, it's equally important to set them in a way that increases your chances of success. Goals should be SMART: Specific, Measurable, Achievable, Relevant, and Time-bound. Specific goals provide clarity on exactly what you're trying to achieve. Measurable goals allow you to track your progress. Achievable goals are realistic given your current circumstances. Relevant goals align with your overall life objectives. Time-bound goals have a clear deadline, creating a sense of urgency and helping you stay on track. It's also crucial to set both short-term and long-term financial goals. Short-term goals, such as building an emergency fund or paying off credit card debt, can provide quick wins that boost your motivation and financial stability. Long-term goals, like saving for retirement or your children's education, ensure you're planning for the future. A mix of both types of goals can help you maintain enthusiasm for your financial plan while also securing your long-term financial well-being.

When setting financial goals, it's important to be flexible and understand that life circumstances can change. While your goals should be challenging, they should also be adaptable. Regular review and adjustment of your goals ensure they remain relevant and achievable as your life evolves. This flexibility can help prevent discouragement if you face setbacks or if your priorities shift over time. It's also worth considering the emotional aspect of financial goals. While many financial objectives are practical in nature, it's important to include goals that are emotionally satisfying as well. These might include saving for experiences that bring joy, such as travel or hobbies, or setting aside money for charitable giving.

Including these types of goals can make your overall financial plan more balanced and fulfilling. In conclusion, setting financial goals is an essential part of achieving financial success and overall life satisfaction. It provides direction, motivation, and a framework for making financial decisions. Goals help you prioritize your spending and saving, measure your progress, and adapt to changing life circumstances. They encourage long-term thinking, improve financial literacy, and can even have positive effects on other areas of your life. By taking the time to set clear, meaningful financial goals, you're investing in your future and taking a crucial step towards financial well-being. Remember, the process of setting and working towards financial goals is ongoing. It requires regular review, adjustment, and commitment. But with persistence and dedication, your financial goals can serve as a powerful tool for creating the life you envision for yourself and your loved ones.

Creating a comprehensive financial plan involves setting short-term, mid-term, and long-term goals, as well as ensuring these goals are realistic and achievable. This approach allows you to address immediate needs while also working towards future aspirations, creating a balanced and effective financial strategy. To begin, it's important to understand the distinctions between these different types of goals and how they work together to form a cohesive financial plan.

Short-term financial goals typically focus on immediate needs and wants, usually within a timeframe of one year or less. These goals are often related to budgeting, saving for specific purchases, or addressing pressing financial concerns. Examples of short-term goals might include creating an emergency fund, paying off credit card debt, saving for a vacation, or making a major purchase like a new appliance. Short-term goals are crucial because they provide quick wins that can boost motivation and improve your immediate financial situation. They also help establish good financial habits that will be beneficial for achieving longer-term objectives.

Mid-term financial goals generally fall within a 1-5 year timeframe. These goals bridge the gap between your immediate needs and your long-term aspirations. Mid-term goals might include saving for a down payment on a house, paying off student loans, starting a business, or saving for a child's education. These goals often require more substantial financial commitments and may involve more complex strategies, such as investing in addition to saving.

Long-term financial goals typically extend beyond five years and often encompass major life objectives. The most common long-term financial goal is saving for retirement, but others might include paying off a mortgage, achieving financial independence, or leaving a legacy for future generations. Long-term goals require careful planning, consistent effort, and often involve more sophisticated financial strategies such as diversified investment portfolios.

When creating these goals, it's essential to make them specific and measurable. Instead of a vague goal like "save more money," a specific short-term goal might be "save $5,000 for an emergency fund in the next six months." For a mid-term goal, you might aim to "save $30,000 for a house down payment in three years." A long-term goal could be "accumulate $1 million in retirement savings by age 65." By quantifying your goals and attaching specific timeframes, you make it easier to track your progress and stay motivated.

To set realistic and achievable goals, start by assessing your current financial situation. This includes calculating your net worth, reviewing your income and expenses, and understanding your cash flow. This assessment will give you a clear picture of where you stand financially and what resources you have available to work towards your goals. Be honest with yourself during this process – understanding your true financial position is crucial for setting goals that are challenging yet attainable.

Next, prioritize your goals based on their importance and urgency. While it's great to have multiple financial objectives, trying to pursue too many goals simultaneously can be overwhelming and may lead to frustration. By prioritizing, you can focus your resources on the most critical goals first. For example, building an emergency fund and paying off high-interest debt might take precedence over saving for a vacation or a new car.

When setting your goals, be sure to consider your personal values and life circumstances. Your financial goals should align with your overall life objectives and what's truly important to you. For instance, if travel is a priority for you, incorporating regular travel savings into your short and mid-term goals might be more meaningful than aggressively paying off a low-interest mortgage.

It's also important to be realistic about the timeframes for your goals. While it's admirable to be ambitious, setting overly aggressive timelines can lead to disappointment and burnout. Consider factors such as your current income, expenses, and saving capacity when determining how quickly you can realistically achieve each goal. It's often better to set a slightly longer timeframe and exceed your expectations than to set an unrealistic deadline and fall short. Another key aspect of setting achievable goals is to break them down into smaller, manageable steps. For instance, if your mid-term goal is to save $30,000 for a house down payment in three years, break that down into an annual savings target of $10,000, then further into a monthly savings goal of about $833. This approach makes the goal less daunting and allows you to track your progress more frequently, providing regular motivation as you hit these smaller milestones.

When creating your financial goals, it's crucial to consider potential obstacles and plan for them. Life is unpredictable, and unexpected expenses or income changes can derail even the best-laid plans. Build some flexibility into your goals and consider creating contingency plans. For example, you might set a slightly lower savings target than you think you can achieve, giving yourself some buffer for unexpected events. It's also important to regularly review and adjust your goals. Your financial situation and priorities may change over time, and your goals should reflect these changes. Set up regular check-ins – perhaps quarterly for short-term goals and annually for mid and long-term goals – to assess your progress and make any necessary adjustments. This ongoing evaluation ensures your goals remain relevant and achievable as your life circumstances evolve.

When setting long-term goals, particularly for major objectives like retirement savings, it's often helpful to work backwards. Start by envisioning your desired outcome – for example, the lifestyle you want in retirement and how much that might cost annually. Then, using reasonable assumptions about inflation and investment returns, calculate how much you need to save and invest now to reach that goal. This approach can help ensure your long-term goals are grounded in reality and give you a clear target to work towards. For mid-term goals, consider how they fit into your overall financial picture. For instance, if you're saving for a house down payment, think about how this goal aligns with your other objectives. Will aggressively saving for a house impact your ability to save for retirement or other long-term goals? Finding the right balance is key to creating a sustainable financial plan. Short-term goals often require a different approach. Since the time frame is shorter, you'll likely focus more on budgeting and saving rather than investing. Look for areas in your current spending where you can cut back to free up money for your short-term goals. You might also consider ways to increase your income in the short term, such as taking on extra hours at work or starting a side hustle.

When setting goals, it's also important to consider the potential trade-offs between different objectives. For example, aggressively paying off low-interest debt might feel good psychologically, but it could come at the expense of investing for retirement, which might offer better long-term financial benefits. Understanding these trade-offs can help you make more informed decisions about how to prioritize your goals. Another crucial aspect of setting achievable financial goals is to educate yourself about personal finance and investment strategies. The more you understand about topics like budgeting, saving, investing, and tax planning, the better equipped you'll be to set realistic goals and develop effective strategies to achieve them. Consider reading personal finance books, attending workshops, or working with a financial advisor to enhance your financial literacy. It's also worth considering the role of automation in achieving your goals. Many financial institutions offer tools to automatically transfer money from your checking account to savings or investment accounts. By automating your savings and investments, you remove the temptation to spend the money elsewhere and ensure consistent progress towards your goals. When setting goals, especially long-term ones, it's important to factor in the impact of inflation. The cost of goods and services typically increases over time, which means the purchasing power of your money decreases. For long-term goals like retirement savings, make sure you're aiming for a target that accounts for the future cost of living, not just today's prices.

It's also crucial to be prepared to make sacrifices to achieve your financial goals. This might mean cutting back on discretionary spending, taking on additional work, or delaying gratification in certain areas of your life. However, it's important to strike a balance – your financial plan should allow for some enjoyment in the present while working towards future goals. Remember that setbacks are a normal part of any financial journey. When setting your goals, build in some room for unexpected events or mistakes. If you fall behind on a goal, don't get discouraged. Instead, reassess your approach and make adjustments as necessary. The ability to adapt and persevere in the face of challenges is key to long-term financial success.

Finally, consider the psychological aspect of goal-setting. Choose goals that are meaningful to you personally, not just ones that you think you should have. When you're emotionally invested in your goals, you're more likely to stay motivated and committed to achieving them. Also, don't underestimate the power of visualizing your goals. Create vision boards, write down your goals, or use other techniques to keep your objectives front and center in your mind. In conclusion, creating short-term, mid-term, and long-term financial goals, and ensuring they are realistic and achievable, is a crucial step in taking control of your financial future. By carefully assessing your current situation, prioritizing your objectives, breaking down larger goals into manageable steps, and regularly reviewing and adjusting your plan, you can create a roadmap for financial success that aligns with your values and life aspirations. Remember, the process of working towards your financial goals is a journey, not a destination. With patience, perseverance, and a willingness to learn and adapt, you can make steady progress towards your financial objectives and build a more secure and fulfilling financial future.

Staying motivated and tracking progress are essential elements in achieving your financial goals. Without consistent motivation, it's easy to lose sight of your objectives and fall back into old spending habits. Similarly, tracking your progress provides tangible evidence of your advancement, which can fuel your motivation and help you stay on course. To maintain motivation, it's crucial to remind yourself regularly of the reasons behind your financial goals. Visualize the end result - whether it's the feeling of financial security, the excitement of a major purchase, or the peace of mind that comes with being debt-free. This emotional connection to your goals can be a powerful motivator when faced with financial decisions or temptations.

One effective strategy for staying motivated is to break down larger financial goals into smaller, more manageable milestones. For instance, if your goal is to save $10,000 for a down payment on a house, celebrate when you reach $1,000, $2,500, and $5,000. These intermediate victories provide a sense of accomplishment and momentum, making the overall goal feel more attainable. Consider setting up small rewards for yourself when you hit these milestones - just ensure that these rewards don't derail your financial progress.

Creating a visual representation of your progress can be incredibly motivating. This could be as simple as a chart on your wall that you color in as you get closer to your goal, or as sophisticated as a spreadsheet with graphs showing your progress over time. The act of physically updating your progress tracker can be satisfying and serves as a regular reminder of how far you've come. Many budgeting apps also offer visual tracking features, which can be particularly appealing to tech-savvy individuals.

Sharing your goals with trusted friends or family members can also help you stay motivated. When you verbalize your objectives to others, you're more likely to feel accountable. Moreover, having a support system that cheers you on and offers encouragement during challenging times can be invaluable. Some people find success in forming or joining money-saving groups or online communities where members share their goals, strategies, and progress.

To effectively track your progress, it's essential to establish clear, measurable benchmarks from the outset. Instead of a vague goal like "save more money," set a specific target like "save $300 per month." This allows you to easily assess whether you're meeting your objectives each month. Use tools like budgeting apps, spreadsheets, or even a simple notebook to record your income, expenses, and savings regularly. Consistency in tracking is key - set aside time each week or month to update your financial records and review your progress.

Another useful strategy is to automate your savings and bill payments as much as possible. This not only ensures consistent progress towards your goals but also simplifies the tracking process. When a portion of your income is automatically directed to savings or investments, you're less likely to spend it elsewhere, and it's easier to see your progress over time.

Regularly reviewing and adjusting your goals is also crucial for maintaining motivation and ensuring your tracking methods remain relevant. As your financial situation or priorities change, your goals may need to evolve as well. Perhaps you've received a raise and can increase your savings rate, or maybe an unexpected expense has necessitated a temporary slowdown in your debt repayment plan. By regularly reassessing your goals and progress, you can make informed adjustments and avoid the discouragement that might come from rigidly sticking to outdated objectives.

It's important to acknowledge that there will likely be setbacks along the way. Perhaps you miss a savings goal one month or have an unexpected expense that slows your progress. Instead of getting discouraged, view these setbacks as learning opportunities. Analyze what went wrong and how you can prevent similar issues in the future. Remember, progress isn't always linear, and small setbacks don't negate the progress you've already made.

Consider using technology to your advantage in both staying motivated and tracking progress. There are numerous apps and online tools designed to help with budgeting, saving, and investing. Many of these offer features like goal setting, progress tracking, and even gamification elements that can make the process more engaging. However, choose tools that you're comfortable using consistently - the best tracking method is the one you'll actually use.

Another motivational technique is to educate yourself about personal finance and investing. The more you understand about how money works, the more confident and motivated you'll likely feel about managing your finances. Read books, listen to podcasts, or take online courses about personal finance. Not only will this knowledge help you make better financial decisions, but it can also make the process of working towards your goals more interesting and engaging.

Remember to celebrate your successes, no matter how small. Acknowledging your progress reinforces positive financial behaviors and provides the emotional boost needed to continue working towards your goals. These celebrations don't need to be expensive - they could be as simple as treating yourself to a favorite home-cooked meal or enjoying a movie night with friends.

When it comes to financial goals for teens, it's important to consider both short-term objectives that provide quick wins and longer-term goals that encourage forward thinking. One common short-term goal for many teens is saving for a car. This goal not only provides a tangible reward but also teaches valuable lessons about saving, budgeting, and delayed gratification.

For a teen saving for a car, the first step is to determine a realistic target. This involves researching car prices, considering whether they're aiming for a new or used vehicle, and factoring in additional costs like insurance, maintenance, and fuel. Let's say a teen decides they want to save $5,000 for a used car within two years. They could break this down into a monthly savings goal of about $208. To achieve this, they might need to get a part-time job or find ways to earn money through babysitting, lawn care, or other side gigs.

Tracking progress towards this car savings goal could involve creating a visual representation, like a picture of their dream car with a savings thermometer next to it. As they save more, they can color in the thermometer, providing a visual reminder of their progress. They might also use a dedicated savings account for their car fund, making it easier to track their growing balance and potentially earn some interest.

To stay motivated, the teen might research different car models within their price range, learning about features and reliability ratings. This not only keeps the goal exciting but also educates them about making informed purchasing decisions. They could also create a budget to manage their income and expenses, ensuring they're setting aside enough for their car fund while still having some money for other priorities.

Another important financial goal for many teens is saving for college. This longer-term goal requires more planning and often involves collaboration with parents or guardians. The first step is to research potential college costs, including tuition, room and board, books, and other expenses. It's also important to explore potential sources of funding like scholarships, grants, and student loans.

Let's say a 15-year-old sets a goal to save $10,000 for college expenses by the time they graduate high school in three years. This might break down to a monthly savings goal of about $278. Achieving this goal likely requires a combination of strategies. The teen might allocate a portion of their earnings from a part-time job or summer employment. They could also save monetary gifts received for birthdays or holidays.

To track progress towards this college savings goal, the teen might use a dedicated college savings account or a 529 plan if available. These accounts not only help separate college savings from other funds but may also offer tax advantages. A spreadsheet or budgeting app could be used to track monthly contributions and overall progress.

Staying motivated for a long-term goal like college savings can be challenging for teens. One strategy is to break the larger goal into smaller, annual targets. For example, aiming to save $3,333 per year feels more manageable than $10,000 over three years. The teen might also research potential careers or majors they're interested in, keeping the end goal of attending college at the forefront of their mind.

Another financial goal for teens might be to start building an emergency fund. While teens typically have fewer financial responsibilities than adults, having a small emergency fund can provide valuable financial lessons and a safety net for unexpected expenses. A teen might set a goal to save $500 or $1,000 in an easily accessible savings account.

To achieve this, they could allocate a small portion of their earnings or allowance each week or month. For example, saving $20 per week would result in $1,040 after a year. Tracking this goal could involve using a simple spreadsheet or even a jar where they physically add money each week, providing a visual representation of their growing emergency fund.

Entrepreneurial teens might set a goal to save money to start a small business or side hustle. This could involve saving for equipment, inventory, or marketing materials. For instance, a teen interested in photography might set a goal to save $1,500 for a quality camera and editing software. They could track their progress using a dedicated savings account or a chart showing their savings growing alongside images of the equipment they plan to purchase.

Some teens might also be interested in learning about investing. A goal could be to save enough to make their first investment, perhaps in a low-cost index fund or a few shares of a company they're interested in. For example, they might set a goal to save $500 to open a custodial investment account. This goal not only encourages saving but also provides an opportunity to learn about the stock market, compound interest, and long-term investing strategies.

To track progress on an investing goal, a teen could use a spreadsheet to record their savings, research potential investments, and eventually track the performance of their investments. Staying motivated might involve learning more about investing through books, podcasts, or reputable online resources.

For teens who are passionate about giving back to their community, a financial goal might involve saving money to donate to a cause they care about. They could set a goal to save a certain amount, like $200, to donate by the end of the year. Tracking could involve a simple chart or savings jar, while motivation could come from learning more about the impact of their potential donation.

Regardless of the specific goal, it's important for teens to understand the concept of opportunity cost - the idea that choosing to save for one goal might mean foregoing something else. This understanding can help them prioritize their goals and make informed decisions about how to allocate their money.

Parents or mentors can play a crucial role in helping teens stay motivated and track their progress towards financial goals. This might involve helping them set up tracking systems, discussing their progress regularly, or even offering incentives like matching contributions to their savings.

In conclusion, staying motivated and tracking progress are vital components of achieving financial goals, whether you're an adult managing multiple financial objectives or a teen saving for your first major purchase. By setting clear, measurable goals, using visual tracking methods, celebrating milestones, and staying educated about personal finance, individuals of all ages can maintain their motivation and make steady progress towards their financial objectives. For teens, early experiences with setting and achieving financial goals can lay the foundation for a lifetime of sound money management skills.

Exercise

Write Down Your Financial Goals and Create a Plan to Achieve Them

Part 1: Identify Your Financial Goals

1. Short-term goals (0-12 months):

Goal 1:

_____

Goal 2:

_____

Goal 3:

_____

2. Mid-term goals (1-5 years):

Goal 1:

_____

Goal 2:

_____

Goal 3:

_____

3. Long-term goals (5+ years):

Goal 1:

_____

Goal 2:

_____

Goal 3:

_____

Part 2: Make Your Goals SMART

For each goal, ensure it is:

- Specific: What exactly do you want to achieve?

- Measurable: How will you track progress?

- Achievable: Is it realistic given your current situation?

- Relevant: Does it align with your values and long-term objectives?

- Time-bound: By when do you want to achieve this goal?

Example:

Original goal: Save money for a car

SMART goal: Save $5,000 for a used car down payment by December 31st next year

Revise your goals to make them SMART:

_____

_____

_____

Part 3: Prioritize Your Goals

Rank your goals in order of importance:

_____

_____

_____

Part 4: Create an Action Plan

For each of your top 3 goals, outline the steps you'll take to achieve them:

Goal 1:

_____

Step 1:

Step 2:

Step 3:

Goal 2:

Step 1:

Step 2:

Step 3:

Goal 3:

Step 1:

Step 2:

Step 3:

Part 5: Identify Potential Obstacles and Solutions

For each goal, list potential obstacles and how you'll overcome them:

Goal 1:

Obstacle:

_____

Solution:

_____

Goal 2:

Obstacle:

_____

Solution:

_____

Goal 3:

Obstacle:

_____

Solution:

_____

Part 6: Determine How You'll Track Progress

For each goal, decide how you'll monitor your advancement:

Goal 1:

_____

Tracking method:

_____

Goal 2:

_____

Tracking method:

_____

Goal 3:

_____

Tracking method:

_____

Part 7: Set Review Dates

Schedule regular times to review your progress and adjust your plan if necessary:

Monthly review date:

_____

Quarterly review date:

_____

Annual review date:

_____

Part 8: Accountability

How will you hold yourself accountable?

Share goals with a friend/family member?

_____

Join a financial support group?

_____

Work with a financial advisor?

_____

Other:

_____

Part 9: Motivation Strategy

List three ways you'll stay motivated:

_____

_____

_____

Part 10: Celebrate Milestones

For each goal, decide how you'll celebrate when you reach important milestones:

Goal 1:

_____

Celebration:

_____

Goal 2:

_____

Celebration:

_____

Goal 3:

_____

Celebration:

_____

Remember, this is a living document. Review and adjust your plan regularly as your circumstances and goals evolve.

Chapter 10

FINANCIAL RESPONSIBILITY AND BUILDING WEALTH

Financial responsibility is a fundamental aspect of personal and professional success that extends far beyond simply managing money. It encompasses a wide range of skills, habits, and attitudes that contribute to long-term financial stability and prosperity. At its core, financial responsibility involves making informed decisions about earning, spending, saving, and investing money in a way that aligns with one's values and goals. It requires a combination of self-discipline, forward-thinking, and a willingness to learn and adapt to changing financial circumstances. The importance of financial responsibility cannot be overstated in today's complex economic landscape. As individuals navigate an increasingly interconnected global economy, they face a myriad of financial challenges and opportunities. Those who cultivate financial responsibility are better equipped to weather economic uncertainties, take advantage of opportunities for growth, and build a secure future for themselves and their loved ones.

Financial responsibility serves as a foundation for achieving personal goals, whether they involve purchasing a home, starting a business, funding education, or planning for retirement. Moreover, financial responsibility extends beyond personal benefits to impact broader society. Individuals who manage their finances responsibly contribute to economic stability by maintaining healthy levels of savings, making informed investment decisions, and avoiding excessive debt. This collective financial responsibility can lead to stronger communities, reduced reliance on social welfare programs, and a more resilient economy overall. Additionally, financially responsible individuals are often better positioned to give back to their communities through charitable contributions and volunteer work, further enhancing social well-being.

Developing financial responsibility is a lifelong journey that begins with education and awareness. It involves understanding basic financial concepts, such as budgeting, saving, and investing, as well as more complex topics like tax planning, risk management, and retirement strategies. Equally important is the development of healthy financial habits, such as living within one's means, avoiding unnecessary debt, and consistently saving for the future. These habits, when cultivated over time, can lead to significant wealth accumulation and financial security. Financial responsibility also entails being proactive about one's financial situation. This means regularly reviewing and adjusting financial plans, staying informed about economic trends and financial products, and seeking professional advice when necessary. It involves taking calculated risks when appropriate while also maintaining a safety net for unexpected expenses or economic downturns. By adopting a proactive approach, individuals can maximize their financial potential and minimize the impact of unforeseen financial challenges. In essence, financial responsibility is about taking control of one's financial life and making choices that support long-term financial health and well-being. It empowers individuals to make confident decisions about their money, reduces financial stress, and provides a sense of security and freedom. As we delve deeper into the concept of financial responsibility and its role in building wealth, we will explore practical strategies, common pitfalls to avoid, and the mindset required to achieve lasting financial success. By embracing financial responsibility, individuals can lay the groundwork for a prosperous future and contribute to a more stable and thriving society.

Developing good financial habits early in life can have a profound impact on an individual's ability to build wealth over time. These habits, when consistently practiced, create a solid foundation for financial success and can lead to significant wealth accumulation in the future. One of the most crucial habits is living below one's means. This involves spending less than you earn and resisting the temptation to indulge in unnecessary expenses. By adopting this mindset, individuals can create a surplus in their budget, which can be directed towards savings and investments. Over time, this consistent saving can grow into substantial wealth through the power of compound interest. Another essential habit is regular and automatic saving. By treating savings as a non-negotiable expense and automating the process, individuals ensure that a portion of their income is consistently set aside for the future. This habit not only builds wealth but also provides a financial buffer for unexpected expenses or economic downturns. Starting this habit early allows more time for investments to grow and compound, potentially leading to significant wealth accumulation over decades. Developing a habit of financial education is equally important. Continuously learning about personal finance, investment strategies, and economic trends equips individuals with the knowledge needed to make informed financial decisions. This ongoing education can lead to better investment choices, more effective tax planning, and a deeper understanding of how to optimize one's financial situation. Over time, this knowledge can translate into substantial financial gains and help individuals navigate complex financial landscapes more effectively.

Cultivating a habit of setting and pursuing financial goals is another key factor in building future wealth. By establishing clear, measurable objectives - such as saving for a home down payment, building an emergency fund, or investing for retirement - individuals create a roadmap for their financial journey. These goals provide motivation and direction, helping to maintain focus on long-term financial success rather than short-term gratification. The habit of tracking expenses and maintaining a budget is fundamental to financial responsibility and wealth building. By consistently monitoring where money is being spent, individuals can identify areas of unnecessary expenditure and redirect those funds towards savings and investments. This habit also fosters awareness of spending patterns, making it easier to make conscious choices about where to allocate resources.

Developing a habit of delayed gratification is crucial for long-term wealth accumulation. This involves resisting the urge to make immediate purchases in favor of saving or investing for the future. By prioritizing long-term financial goals over short-term desires, individuals can allocate more resources towards wealth-building activities. Another valuable habit is regular financial check-ups. This involves periodically reviewing one's financial situation, including income, expenses, debts, and investments. By making this a regular practice, individuals can ensure they stay on track with their financial goals, make necessary adjustments, and identify new opportunities for wealth creation.

The habit of diversifying investments is essential for building sustainable wealth. This involves spreading investments across different asset classes, sectors, and geographic regions to minimize risk and maximize potential returns. By consistently practicing diversification, individuals can protect their wealth from market volatility and potentially enhance long-term returns. Developing a habit of seeking professional advice when needed is another important aspect of building future wealth. While it's essential to educate oneself about personal finance, there are times when the expertise of financial professionals can provide valuable insights and strategies. Making a habit of consulting with financial advisors, tax professionals, or legal experts when facing complex financial decisions can lead to better outcomes and potentially significant financial benefits over time.

Cultivating a positive mindset towards money and wealth is a habit that can significantly impact future financial success. This involves viewing money as a tool for achieving goals and creating opportunities rather than a source of stress or anxiety. A positive money mindset can lead to more proactive financial behaviors and a greater willingness to take calculated risks that may result in substantial rewards. While developing good financial habits is crucial for building future wealth, it's equally important to avoid common pitfalls that can derail financial progress. One such pitfall is lifestyle inflation, which occurs when an individual's spending increases in proportion to their rising income. This phenomenon can significantly hinder wealth accumulation and financial security if not properly managed. Lifestyle inflation often occurs subtly and gradually. As individuals earn more money, they may feel entitled to upgrade their lifestyle, justifying increased spending on luxury items, larger homes, newer cars, or more expensive vacations. While some lifestyle improvements are natural and can contribute to overall life satisfaction, unchecked lifestyle inflation can prevent individuals from capitalizing on their increased earning potential to build wealth.

To avoid falling into the trap of lifestyle inflation, it's essential to maintain perspective on one's financial goals and priorities. When income increases, whether through a raise, promotion, or new job opportunity, it's crucial to resist the immediate urge to increase spending. Instead, individuals should consider allocating a significant portion of the additional income towards savings, investments, or debt repayment. This approach allows for the acceleration of wealth-building efforts while still potentially allowing for some modest lifestyle improvements.

One effective strategy for avoiding lifestyle inflation is to adhere to the principle of "paying yourself first." This involves immediately directing a portion of any income increase towards savings or investments before considering any lifestyle upgrades. By automating this process, individuals can ensure that their wealth-building efforts scale with their income, rather than being consumed by increased spending. Another important aspect of avoiding lifestyle inflation is maintaining a long-term perspective. It's easy to justify increased spending in the present moment, especially when peers or colleagues may be visibly upgrading their lifestyles. However, keeping focus on long-term financial goals, such as early retirement, financial independence, or funding children's education, can provide the motivation needed to resist short-term spending temptations. Practicing gratitude and contentment with one's current lifestyle can also be a powerful tool in combating lifestyle inflation. By appreciating what one already has and finding satisfaction in non-material aspects of life, individuals can reduce the psychological pull towards constant lifestyle upgrades. This doesn't mean never improving one's living situation, but rather making conscious, intentional choices about when and how to do so, always in alignment with broader financial goals. It's also important to be mindful of the hidden costs associated with lifestyle inflation. Upgrading to a larger home, for instance, often comes with increased property taxes, higher utility bills, and more expensive maintenance costs. Similarly, purchasing a luxury car may entail higher insurance premiums and costlier repairs. By considering these hidden costs, individuals can make more informed decisions about potential lifestyle changes and their long-term financial implications.

One effective strategy for managing lifestyle inflation is to create a "lifestyle cap." This involves setting a limit on the percentage of income allocated to lifestyle expenses, regardless of income increases. For example, an individual might decide to cap their lifestyle spending at 50% of their income, with the remainder going towards savings, investments, and other financial goals. As income rises, the absolute amount available for lifestyle expenses would increase, but the percentage would remain constant, ensuring that a significant portion of income growth is directed towards wealth-building activities. Another approach to mitigating lifestyle inflation is to focus on value-based spending. This involves aligning spending decisions with personal values and long-term goals, rather than societal expectations or short-term desires. By prioritizing expenditures that truly enhance quality of life or contribute to personal growth, individuals can avoid unnecessary lifestyle inflation while still enjoying the benefits of increased income.

It's also crucial to be aware of the role of social influences in driving lifestyle inflation. Social media, advertising, and peer pressure can create a sense of needing to "keep up with the Joneses." Recognizing these influences and consciously evaluating their impact on personal financial decisions is essential for maintaining control over spending habits.

Developing a habit of delayed gratification can be particularly effective in combating lifestyle inflation. By learning to postpone non-essential purchases and carefully considering the long-term impact of spending decisions, individuals can avoid impulsive upgrades that may not align with their financial goals. This doesn't mean never enjoying the fruits of one's labor, but rather making thoughtful, intentional choices about when and how to do so. Another important consideration in avoiding lifestyle inflation is the concept of hedonic adaptation. This psychological phenomenon suggests that humans quickly adapt to improvements in their circumstances, returning to a baseline level of happiness. Understanding this concept can help individuals resist the urge to constantly upgrade their lifestyle in pursuit of happiness, recognizing that such upgrades often provide only temporary satisfaction. It's also worth noting that some degree of lifestyle inflation can be appropriate and even beneficial, particularly when it involves investments in personal health, education, or experiences that contribute to long-term well-being and earning potential. The key is to approach such upgrades strategically, always considering their alignment with overall financial goals and values.

Regularly reassessing one's lifestyle choices and their alignment with financial goals is crucial for avoiding unchecked lifestyle inflation. This might involve periodically reviewing spending patterns, evaluating the true value derived from various expenditures, and making adjustments as necessary. By maintaining this level of awareness and intentionality, individuals can ensure that their lifestyle remains in harmony with their long-term financial objectives. In conclusion, developing good financial habits and avoiding lifestyle inflation are crucial elements in building long-term wealth. By consistently practicing habits such as living below one's means, regular saving, continuous financial education, and mindful spending, individuals can create a strong foundation for future financial success. Simultaneously, by being aware of the pitfalls of lifestyle inflation and implementing strategies to mitigate its effects, individuals can ensure that increases in income translate into accelerated wealth accumulation rather than increased consumption. The combination of positive financial habits and controlled lifestyle inflation can lead to significant wealth building over time, providing financial security, freedom, and the ability to pursue life goals with confidence. Remember, building wealth is not just about earning more money, but about making smart choices with the money you have and consistently aligning your financial decisions with your long-term objectives.

Philanthropy and giving back play a significant role in the realm of financial responsibility and wealth building. While it may seem counterintuitive to discuss giving money away in the context of accumulating wealth, philanthropy is often an integral part of a well-rounded financial strategy. For many wealthy individuals, the ability to make a positive impact on society through charitable giving is not only a moral imperative but also a source of personal fulfillment and legacy building. The act of giving back can take many forms, from monetary donations to volunteering time and expertise. For those building wealth, incorporating philanthropy into their financial plan can provide numerous benefits. Firstly, it allows individuals to support causes they care about, potentially making a significant difference in areas such as education, healthcare, environmental protection, or social justice. This sense of purpose and contribution can bring a deep sense of satisfaction and meaning to one's financial journey.

Moreover, philanthropy can also offer tangible financial benefits. In many countries, charitable donations are tax-deductible, which can help reduce an individual's overall tax burden. Strategic charitable giving can be an effective tool in tax planning, allowing wealthy individuals to direct their money towards causes they support rather than paying it in taxes. However, it's important to note that true philanthropy is motivated by a genuine desire to make a positive impact, not solely by tax benefits. Philanthropy can also be a powerful tool for teaching future generations about financial responsibility and the importance of giving back. Wealthy individuals often involve their children in philanthropic activities, helping them develop a sense of social responsibility and an understanding of the privileges and obligations that come with wealth. This can be a valuable part of passing on not just financial assets, but also values and a sense of purpose to the next generation.

For many successful entrepreneurs and business leaders, philanthropy becomes a second career or a major focus later in life. Notable examples include Bill Gates and Warren Buffett, who have pledged to give away the majority of their wealth to charitable causes. Their Giving Pledge initiative has inspired many other billionaires to make similar commitments, potentially redirecting trillions of dollars towards addressing global challenges. Philanthropy can also play a role in building social capital and expanding networks. Involvement in charitable organizations often brings individuals into contact with like-minded peers, potentially leading to new business opportunities, partnerships, or collaborations. While this should not be the primary motivation for giving, it's an additional benefit that can contribute to ongoing wealth building and personal growth. It's worth noting that effective philanthropy requires the same level of strategic thinking and due diligence as any other financial decision. Wealthy individuals often create structured giving plans, thoroughly researching potential recipient organizations to ensure their donations will have the maximum impact. Some establish their own foundations or donor-advised funds to have more control over how their charitable contributions are used.

The concept of impact investing has also gained traction in recent years, blurring the lines between philanthropy and traditional investing. This approach involves making investments with the intention of generating both financial returns and positive social or environmental impact. For wealth builders who are passionate about certain causes, impact investing can be a way to align their investment portfolio with their values while still working towards financial goals. As individuals build wealth, they often find that their capacity for giving increases. This can lead to a virtuous cycle where financial success enables greater philanthropy, which in turn brings personal fulfillment and potentially opens up new opportunities for further success. Many wealthy individuals report that their philanthropic activities bring them as much or more satisfaction than their business endeavors.

However, it's important to approach philanthropy responsibly and sustainably. Just as with personal finances, it's crucial not to overextend oneself in charitable giving. A balanced approach ensures that individuals can continue to build and maintain their wealth while also making meaningful contributions to causes they care about. For those in the early stages of wealth building, starting small with philanthropy can be a good way to develop the habit of giving back. This might involve setting aside a small percentage of income for charitable donations, volunteering time for local organizations, or participating in workplace giving programs. As wealth grows, these philanthropic efforts can be scaled up accordingly.

Ultimately, the role of philanthropy in wealth building is about creating a holistic approach to financial success – one that recognizes the interconnectedness of personal prosperity and societal well-being. By incorporating giving back into their financial strategies, individuals can work towards building wealth in a way that not only benefits themselves but also contributes to the greater good.

Turning to examples of wealthy individuals who started with smart money habits, there are numerous inspiring stories of people who built significant wealth through disciplined financial practices. These examples demonstrate that while factors like innovation, market timing, and sometimes luck play a role in extreme wealth accumulation, the foundation is often laid by solid financial habits developed early on.

One of the most well-known examples is Warren Buffett, often referred to as the "Oracle of Omaha." Buffett's wealth-building journey began with small, smart financial decisions in his youth. He started working and saving money at a young age, delivering newspapers and selling chewing gum door-to-door. By the time he was a teenager, Buffett had already started investing in stocks and had filed his first tax return. His habit of living below his means, even as his wealth grew astronomically, is legendary. Buffett still lives in the same house he bought in 1958 for $31,500, despite being one of the wealthiest people in the world. His approach to investing – focusing on value and holding for the long term – has been consistent throughout his career. Another example is Charlie Munger, Buffett's long-time business partner. Munger, like Buffett, developed strong financial habits early in life. He worked multiple jobs as a teenager and young adult, saving diligently. Munger is known for his emphasis on continuous learning and his multidisciplinary approach to decision-making, which he applies to both investing and personal finance. His habit of "inverting" problems – thinking about what to avoid rather than what to pursue – has been a key factor in his financial success.

Oprah Winfrey's journey to wealth also began with smart money habits developed in the face of early financial hardship. Growing up in poverty, Winfrey learned the value of hard work and financial discipline from a young age. As her career in media took off, she made a point of saving and investing a significant portion of her earnings. Winfrey has spoken about the importance of living below one's means and avoiding lifestyle inflation. Even as she became one of the wealthiest women in the world, she maintained a focus on smart financial management and strategic business decisions. Self-made billionaire Mark Cuban attributes much of his success to habits he developed in his youth. Cuban started his entrepreneurial journey early, selling garbage bags door-to-door as a teenager. He has spoken about the importance of living frugally in his early adult years, sharing an apartment with several roommates and eating cheap meals to save money. Cuban emphasizes the importance of continual learning and being willing to work harder than anyone else – habits that served him well as he built his businesses and investment portfolio.

Sara Blakely, the founder of Spanx and the youngest self-made female billionaire, also credits smart money habits for her success. Before starting her company, Blakely worked in sales and developed a habit of saving a significant portion of her income. She famously bootstrapped Spanx with $5,000 of her own savings, running the company out of her apartment to keep costs low. Blakely's emphasis on frugality in both her personal life and business operations allowed her to grow Spanx without taking on outside investment, maintaining full ownership of the company. John Paul DeJoria, co-founder of Paul Mitchell hair products and Patrón tequila, built his fortune from a background of extreme poverty. DeJoria's early financial habits were born out of necessity – he was homeless twice before finding success. He learned to live on very little and to save whatever he could. Even after achieving success, DeJoria maintained these frugal habits, focusing on building his businesses rather than lavish personal spending.

Carlos Slim, once the richest person in the world, developed his financial acumen at a young age. He started investing in government savings bonds as a child and kept detailed financial records in a ledger. Slim is known for his frugal personal habits, despite his immense wealth. He has lived in the same house for decades and drives himself rather than employing a chauffeur. His approach to business and investing emphasizes patience, thorough analysis, and a long-term perspective. Jeff Bezos, founder of Amazon, started his company with savings from his previous job and investments from family members. In the early days of Amazon, Bezos was known for his frugality, using doors as desks to save money. This focus on cost-cutting and reinvesting profits back into the business was a key factor in Amazon's growth. Even as his personal wealth grew, Bezos maintained a focus on long-term value creation rather than short-term profits or personal expenditure.

These examples demonstrate several common themes in the habits of individuals who have built significant wealth:

1. Starting early: Many of these individuals began developing smart financial habits in childhood or early adulthood.

2. Living below means: Consistently spending less than they earned allowed these individuals to save and invest aggressively.

3. Continuous learning: A commitment to ongoing education and skill development is a common trait among self-made wealthy individuals.

4. Long-term perspective: These wealth builders focused on long-term value creation rather than short-term gains or luxuries.

5. Reinvestment: Many chose to reinvest profits back into their businesses or investment portfolios rather than increasing personal spending.

6. Frugality: Even after achieving significant wealth, many maintained frugal personal habits.

7. Hard work and persistence: A willingness to work harder than others and persist in the face of challenges is a recurring theme.

8. Smart risk-taking: While these individuals were often frugal, they were also willing to take calculated risks when opportunities arose.

It's important to note that while these habits were crucial to these individuals' success, factors such as timing, innovation, and sometimes luck also played roles in their extreme wealth accumulation. However, the foundational financial habits they developed early on positioned them to capitalize on opportunities when they arose.

For those aspiring to build wealth, these examples provide valuable lessons. While not everyone will become a billionaire, adopting similar habits can significantly improve one's financial situation over time. Starting to save and invest early, living below one's means, continuously educating oneself about finance and business, and maintaining a long-term perspective are habits that can benefit anyone, regardless of their current financial situation. Moreover, these examples highlight that building wealth is often a gradual process that requires patience and consistency. It's not about getting rich quickly, but about making smart financial decisions consistently over time. By developing and maintaining good financial habits, individuals can work towards building wealth and achieving their financial goals, while also potentially positioning themselves to give back and make a positive impact on society.

Exercise

Reflect on Your Money Values and How They Align with Your Goals

Part 1: Identify Your Money Values

1. List your top 5 personal values in general:

_____

_____

_____

_____

_____

2. Now, consider how these values might translate to your relationship with money.

Write down 5 money-related values that are important to you:

_____

_____

_____

_____

_____

(Examples might include: financial security, generosity, independence, growth, freedom, etc.)

Part 2: Examine Your Current Financial Behavior

3. List 3-5 recent financial decisions you've made:

_____

_____

_____

_____

_____

4. For each decision, note which of your money values it reflects (if any):

_____

_____

_____

_____

_____

Part 3: Align Values with Goals

5. List your current top 3 financial goals:

_____

_____

_____

6. For each goal, identify which of your money values it supports:

Goal a: Values:

_____

Goal b: Values:

_____

Goal c: Values:

_____

7. Are there any conflicts between your goals and your values? If so, describe them:

_____

_____

_____

Part 4: Value-Based Decision Making

8. Think of an upcoming financial decision you need to make.

Describe it briefly:

_____

_____

9. List the money values that should guide this decision:

_____

_____

10. Outline how you can make this decision in a way that aligns with these values:

_____

_____

_____

Part 5: Philanthropy and Giving

11. Do any of your money values relate to giving or philanthropy? If so, which ones?

_____

_____

12. List 2-3 ways you could incorporate giving into your financial plan that align with your values:

_____

_____

_____

Part 6: Reflection and Action

13. Are there any areas where your current financial behavior doesn't align with your stated money values? Describe them:

_____

_____

_____

14. List 3 specific actions you can take to better align your financial behavior with your money values:

_____

_____

_____

15. How might aligning your financial decisions more closely with your values impact your long-term wealth building?

_____

_____

_____

Reflect on what you've learned about your money values and how they relate to your financial goals. Remember, there's no universally "right" set of money values – what's important is that your financial decisions align with what's truly important to you. Use this exercise as a starting point for making more value-aligned financial decisions in the future.

CONCLUSION: TAKE CHARGE OF YOUR FINANCIAL FUTURE

As we reach the conclusion of this comprehensive guide to personal finance and wealth building, it's important to take a moment to recap the key points we've covered throughout this journey. This book has been designed to provide you with a solid foundation in financial literacy, equipping you with the knowledge and tools necessary to make informed decisions about your money and work towards a secure financial future. We began by emphasizing the importance of financial literacy in today's complex economic landscape. Understanding basic financial concepts is no longer optional but a crucial life skill that impacts every aspect of our lives. From managing daily expenses to planning for retirement, financial literacy empowers individuals to take control of their financial destinies and make choices that align with their long-term goals and values. One of the fundamental concepts we explored was budgeting. We learned that a budget is not a restrictive tool designed to limit enjoyment, but rather a powerful instrument that provides clarity and control over one's finances. We discussed various budgeting methods, from the simple 50/30/20 rule to more detailed zero-based budgeting, emphasizing the importance of finding a system that works for your individual needs and lifestyle.

The key takeaway was that consistent budgeting allows you to align your spending with your priorities, identify areas for potential savings, and make progress towards your financial goals. Closely related to budgeting, we delved into the critical skill of distinguishing between needs and wants. This distinction forms the basis of sound financial decision-making, enabling individuals to prioritize their spending and avoid unnecessary financial strain. We acknowledged that the line between needs and wants can sometimes be blurry and subjective, but emphasized the importance of honest self-reflection in making these determinations. The power of saving was another central theme of our discussions. We explored various savings strategies, from building an emergency fund to saving for specific short-term and long-term goals. The concept of "paying yourself first" was introduced as a powerful habit that can significantly impact long-term financial health. We also discussed the importance of choosing the right savings vehicles for different objectives, considering factors such as liquidity, interest rates, and risk.

Investing was presented as a crucial component of long-term wealth building. We covered the basics of different investment vehicles, including stocks, bonds, mutual funds, and exchange-traded funds (ETFs). The importance of understanding risk tolerance, diversification, and the power of compound interest was emphasized. We also touched on more advanced concepts such as asset allocation and rebalancing, providing a foundation for those interested in developing more sophisticated investment strategies. The topic of debt management was addressed comprehensively, recognizing that not all debt is created equal. We discussed the difference between good debt (such as a mortgage or student loans that can increase earning potential) and bad debt (such as high-interest credit card balances). Strategies for effective debt repayment were explored, including the debt snowball and debt avalanche methods. The importance of avoiding predatory lending and understanding the true cost of borrowing was also highlighted. Credit and its impact on financial health was another key area of focus. We explored the factors that influence credit scores, the importance of regularly checking credit reports, and strategies for building and maintaining good credit. The role of credit in major life decisions, such as renting an apartment, buying a home, or even securing employment, was discussed to underscore its far-reaching implications.

Retirement planning was presented as a critical long-term financial goal. We discussed the importance of starting to save for retirement early to take advantage of compound interest, and explored various retirement savings vehicles such as 401(k)s and IRAs. The concept of estimating retirement needs and developing a strategy to meet those needs was introduced, along with the importance of regularly reviewing and adjusting retirement plans as circumstances change. Insurance was covered as an essential component of a comprehensive financial plan. We discussed various types of insurance, including health, life, disability, and property insurance, emphasizing the role of insurance in protecting against financial catastrophe.

The importance of regularly reviewing insurance coverage to ensure it aligns with current needs and circumstances was stressed. Tax planning was introduced as a strategy for legally minimizing tax liability and maximizing after-tax income. We explored concepts such as tax-advantaged savings accounts, the impact of different types of income on tax liability, and the potential benefits of charitable giving from a tax perspective. The importance of staying informed about tax laws and seeking professional advice when needed was emphasized. The psychological aspects of money management were also addressed. We explored common behavioral biases that can impact financial decision-making, such as loss aversion and overconfidence, and discussed strategies for overcoming these biases. The importance of developing a healthy relationship with money and aligning financial decisions with personal values was emphasized.

Financial goal setting was presented as a crucial step in achieving financial success. We discussed the importance of setting SMART (Specific, Measurable, Achievable, Relevant, Time-bound) goals and breaking larger financial objectives into smaller, manageable steps. The value of regularly reviewing and adjusting goals as circumstances change was emphasized. The concept of financial responsibility was explored in depth, emphasizing that it extends beyond mere money management to encompass a broader sense of stewardship over one's resources. We discussed how financial responsibility involves making informed decisions, considering the long-term implications of financial choices, and balancing personal financial health with broader social and environmental considerations. The role of continuous learning in financial success was a recurring theme throughout the book. We emphasized the importance of staying informed about economic trends, new financial products, and changes in tax laws. The value of seeking advice from financial professionals when needed was discussed, along with strategies for evaluating and choosing trustworthy advisors.

We also explored the concept of financial independence, discussing various approaches to achieving it, from traditional retirement savings to more aggressive strategies like the FIRE (Financial Independence, Retire Early) movement. The importance of defining what financial independence means on a personal level and developing a plan to achieve it was emphasized. The impact of major life events on finances was addressed, covering topics such as marriage, divorce, having children, buying a home, and caring for aging parents. We discussed the importance of planning for these events and adjusting financial strategies accordingly.

Entrepreneurship and its potential for wealth building was explored, discussing both the opportunities and risks associated with starting and running a business. We covered basic concepts of business finance and emphasized the importance of separating personal and business finances. The role of philanthropy in a comprehensive financial plan was discussed, exploring how giving can align with personal values and potentially offer tax benefits. We emphasized the importance of balancing charitable giving with personal financial security and discussed strategies for effective and impactful giving.

Throughout the book, we provided practical exercises and actionable steps to help readers apply the concepts to their personal financial situations. These included budgeting exercises, goal-setting worksheets, and reflective activities designed to help readers clarify their financial values and priorities. In conclusion, this book has aimed to provide a comprehensive overview of personal finance and wealth building strategies. The key message throughout has been that financial success is not about getting rich quickly, but about making informed, consistent decisions aligned with personal goals and values. It's about developing good financial habits, continuously educating oneself, and taking a long-term perspective on financial health and wealth building. Remember, personal finance is just that – personal. While the principles and strategies discussed in this book provide a solid foundation, it's important to adapt them to your individual circumstances, goals, and values. Financial management is an ongoing process that requires regular attention, adjustment, and learning. As you move forward on your financial journey, keep in mind that setbacks and mistakes are normal and can be valuable learning experiences. The key is to stay committed to your long-term financial goals, remain flexible in your approach, and be willing to seek help when needed. Ultimately, the goal of sound financial management is not just to accumulate wealth, but to create a life of financial security, freedom, and fulfillment. By applying the principles and strategies outlined in this book, you are taking important steps towards achieving that goal. Remember, every financial decision you make is an opportunity to move closer to your ideal financial future. Here's to your financial success and the exciting journey ahead!

Continuing to build on your financial knowledge is a crucial aspect of long-term financial success. The world of finance is constantly evolving, with new investment products, changing tax laws, and shifting economic conditions. Staying informed and continuously expanding your financial knowledge allows you to make better decisions, adapt to new opportunities, and navigate potential challenges more effectively. One of the most accessible ways to continue building your financial knowledge is through reading. There are numerous books on personal finance, investing, and economics that can deepen your understanding of various financial concepts. From classics like "The Intelligent Investor" by Benjamin Graham to more recent works like "The Psychology of Money" by Morgan Housel, there's a wealth of knowledge available in book form. Make it a habit to read at least one finance-related book every few months, alternating between different topics to broaden your understanding. In addition to books, staying up-to-date with financial news is crucial. Subscribe to reputable financial news sources such as The Wall Street Journal, Financial Times, or Bloomberg. These publications provide insights into current economic trends, market movements, and policy changes that can impact your financial decisions. However, it's important to approach financial news with a critical eye and a long-term perspective, avoiding the temptation to make impulsive decisions based on short-term market fluctuations.

Online resources can also be invaluable for ongoing financial education. Many financial institutions and investment firms offer free educational resources on their websites, covering topics from basic budgeting to advanced investment strategies. Websites like Investopedia provide a wealth of information on financial terms and concepts, while government websites like the SEC's Investor.gov offer unbiased educational materials and tools. Podcasts have become an increasingly popular medium for financial education. They offer the advantage of being consumable during commutes or while doing other tasks. Look for podcasts that align with your interests and financial goals, whether that's personal finance basics, investing strategies, or economic analysis.

Attending financial seminars and workshops can provide more in-depth learning opportunities. Many local banks, community centers, and universities offer free or low-cost financial education seminars. These events not only provide valuable information but also offer the chance to ask questions and interact with financial professionals and like-minded individuals. For those looking for more structured learning, consider taking online courses in finance or economics. Platforms like Coursera and edX offer courses from top universities, many of which can be audited for free. These courses can provide a more comprehensive understanding of financial concepts and may even lead to professional certifications. Joining investment clubs or financial discussion groups can be another effective way to expand your knowledge. These groups often meet regularly to discuss investment strategies, share insights, and sometimes pool resources for collective investing. The collaborative learning environment can expose you to diverse perspectives and strategies you might not have considered on your own.

For those who prefer a more hands-on approach to learning, consider using stock market simulators or fantasy trading platforms. These tools allow you to practice investing strategies without risking real money, providing valuable experience in a low-stakes environment. As your financial knowledge grows, you may find it beneficial to seek out a financial mentor. This could be a successful investor, a financial professional, or someone you know who has achieved the kind of financial success you aspire to. A mentor can provide personalized advice, share their experiences, and help you avoid common pitfalls. Remember that building financial knowledge is not just about accumulating information, but also about developing critical thinking skills. As you learn, practice analyzing financial information, questioning assumptions, and considering multiple perspectives before making decisions. Lastly, one of the most effective ways to build financial knowledge is through personal experience. While it's important to learn from others, there's no substitute for the lessons learned through managing your own finances. Reflect on your financial decisions, both successful and unsuccessful, and use these experiences to refine your approach over time.

Transitioning to the importance of maintaining good money habits throughout life, it's crucial to understand that financial success is not a destination, but a lifelong journey. The habits and disciplines you develop play a critical role in shaping your financial future. Consistency in applying sound financial principles over time is often more important than making a few big financial decisions. One of the most fundamental habits to maintain is living below your means. This principle remains crucial regardless of your income level or stage of life. As your income grows over time, it can be tempting to increase your spending proportionally. However, maintaining a gap between your income and expenses allows you to continue saving and investing, building wealth over the long term. This habit also provides a buffer against financial shocks and gives you the flexibility to take advantage of opportunities as they arise. Regular budgeting and tracking of expenses is another habit that should be maintained throughout life. As your financial situation evolves – perhaps with changes in income, family size, or living situation – your budget should be adjusted accordingly. The specific method of budgeting may change over time, but the practice of mindful spending and aligning your expenses with your priorities should remain constant. Consistent saving is a habit that pays dividends throughout life. Whether it's for short-term goals, emergencies, or long-term objectives like retirement, the habit of setting aside a portion of your income should be maintained. As your income increases, consider increasing the percentage you save rather than simply increasing your spending.

Regularly reviewing and rebalancing your investment portfolio is a habit that becomes increasingly important as your wealth grows. Markets change, your risk tolerance may shift, and your financial goals may evolve. By making it a habit to review your investments periodically (perhaps annually or semi-annually), you ensure that your investment strategy remains aligned with your current situation and objectives. Staying out of high-interest debt is a habit that can significantly impact your long-term financial health. While some debt, like a mortgage or student loans, can be tools for building wealth, high-interest consumer debt can be a major obstacle to financial progress. Make it a lifelong habit to use credit responsibly and avoid carrying balances on high-interest credit cards. Continuous learning, as discussed earlier, should also be maintained as a lifelong habit. The financial landscape is always changing, and staying informed allows you to make better decisions and adapt to new circumstances. Make it a habit to dedicate time regularly to expanding your financial knowledge.

Practicing delayed gratification is a habit that can serve you well throughout life. In a world of instant satisfaction, the ability to postpone immediate pleasures for long-term benefits is a powerful financial skill. This doesn't mean never enjoying the fruits of your labor, but rather making conscious choices about when and how to indulge, always with an eye on your longer-term financial goals. Regular financial check-ups are another crucial habit to maintain. This involves periodically reviewing your overall financial situation – your income, expenses, debts, investments, insurance coverage, and progress towards goals. By making this a regular practice, perhaps annually, you can identify areas that need attention and make necessary adjustments before small issues become major problems. Maintaining good communication about money, especially with family members or partners, is a habit that can prevent many financial conflicts and ensure that you're working together towards common goals. Regular "money talks" can help keep everyone on the same page and allow for collaborative decision-making on financial matters.

The habit of giving, whether through charitable donations or helping family and friends, is one that many financially successful individuals maintain throughout their lives. Not only can this be personally fulfilling, but it can also provide tax benefits and help maintain a healthy perspective on the role of money in one's life. Avoiding lifestyle inflation as your income grows is a habit that can significantly impact your long-term financial success. While it's natural to want to improve your standard of living as you earn more, maintaining some level of frugality can allow you to accelerate your savings and wealth building. Preparing for the unexpected is a habit that involves maintaining adequate insurance coverage, keeping estate planning documents up to date, and having contingency plans for potential financial setbacks. This habit provides peace of mind and financial protection throughout life. The habit of setting and regularly reviewing financial goals should be maintained throughout your life. As your circumstances change, your goals may need to be adjusted, but the practice of working towards specific financial objectives provides direction and motivation for your financial efforts. Maintaining a long-term perspective is a habit that can help you navigate the ups and downs of financial markets and life events. By focusing on your long-term financial health rather than short-term fluctuations, you can avoid making impulsive decisions based on temporary circumstances.

Practicing gratitude for what you have, rather than constantly focusing on what you lack, is a habit that can lead to greater financial satisfaction and reduce the temptation for unnecessary spending. This mindset can help maintain good financial habits even as your wealth grows. Finally, the habit of taking personal responsibility for your financial decisions is crucial. While it's important to seek advice when needed, ultimately, you are responsible for your financial choices. Maintaining this mindset encourages careful decision-making and continuous learning. Building financial knowledge and maintaining good money habits are interconnected lifelong practices. The knowledge you gain informs the habits you develop, and these habits, in turn, create experiences that deepen your financial understanding. By committing to ongoing learning and consistently applying sound financial principles, you set yourself up for long-term financial success and the ability to navigate whatever financial challenges and opportunities life may bring. Remember, financial management is not about perfection, but about making informed decisions consistently over time. Every day presents new opportunities to learn, to make good choices, and to move closer to your financial goals. Embrace this journey of continuous improvement, and you'll be well-equipped to build and maintain financial health throughout your life.

As we conclude this comprehensive journey through the world of personal finance and wealth building, it's crucial to address the importance of staying motivated and committed to making smart financial decisions. The path to financial success is not always easy or straightforward, but with persistence, dedication, and the right mindset, you can achieve your financial goals and build the life you envision for yourself and your loved ones. One of the key factors in maintaining motivation on your financial journey is to keep your long-term goals firmly in mind. It's easy to get caught up in day-to-day financial decisions and lose sight of the bigger picture. Take time regularly to visualize your financial goals – whether that's a comfortable retirement, financial independence, owning your dream home, or providing for your family's future. This visualization can serve as a powerful motivator when you're faced with financial challenges or temptations to deviate from your plan. Remember that financial success is rarely achieved overnight. It's the result of consistent, small actions taken over time. Each time you make a smart financial decision – whether it's sticking to your budget, increasing your savings rate, or resisting an unnecessary purchase – you're taking a step towards your goals. Celebrate these small victories along the way. They may seem insignificant in the moment, but over time, they add up to significant progress. It's also important to acknowledge that setbacks are a normal part of any financial journey. You may face unexpected expenses, investment losses, or periods of reduced income. Don't let these setbacks discourage you or derail your long-term plans. Instead, view them as learning opportunities. Analyze what went wrong, adjust your strategy if necessary, and move forward with renewed determination. Resilience in the face of financial challenges is a key characteristic of those who achieve lasting financial success.

Staying educated and informed is another crucial aspect of maintaining motivation and making smart financial decisions. The world of finance is constantly evolving, with new investment opportunities, changing tax laws, and shifting economic conditions. Make a commitment to lifelong financial learning. This doesn't mean you need to become a financial expert, but regularly educating yourself about personal finance topics will help you make more informed decisions and feel more confident in your financial path. Consider finding a financial mentor or joining a community of like-minded individuals who are also on a journey of financial improvement. Having support and accountability can be incredibly motivating. Share your goals with trusted friends or family members who can encourage you and check in on your progress. Online forums and local meetups can also be great resources for connecting with others who share your financial aspirations. It's also important to maintain a balanced approach to your finances. While it's crucial to be disciplined and focused on your financial goals, it's equally important to allow for enjoyment and quality of life in the present. Extreme frugality or obsessive saving can lead to burnout and resentment. Find a balance that allows you to make progress towards your long-term goals while still enjoying life in the present. This might mean allocating a portion of your budget for entertainment or travel, or allowing yourself small indulgences that bring joy without derailing your financial plan. Remember that financial decisions are deeply personal and should align with your values and priorities. What works for someone else may not be the right approach for you. Take the time to reflect on what truly matters to you and ensure that your financial decisions support these values. When your financial choices align with your personal values, you're more likely to feel satisfied and motivated to stick with your plan.

Tracking your progress can be a powerful motivational tool. Regularly review your financial situation – your net worth, debt reduction, savings growth, or progress towards specific goals. Seeing tangible evidence of your progress can be incredibly encouraging and can help you stay committed during challenging times. Consider using financial tracking apps or creating your own spreadsheets to visualize your progress over time. It's also important to be patient with yourself and your financial journey. Significant financial changes often take time to manifest. If you find yourself feeling frustrated with the pace of your progress, remind yourself that you're playing a long game. Small, consistent actions compound over time, leading to significant results. Trust in the process and stay committed to your plan. Flexibility is another key component of staying motivated and making smart financial decisions. Life is unpredictable, and your financial plan should be adaptable to changing circumstances. Regularly review and adjust your financial goals and strategies as needed. This flexibility allows you to respond to new opportunities or challenges without feeling like you've failed or need to abandon your plan entirely. Consider the power of automation in maintaining good financial habits. Set up automatic transfers to your savings and investment accounts, automate bill payments, and use technology to track your spending. These automated systems can help you stay on track with your financial goals even during times when your motivation might waver. Remember that financial success is not just about accumulating wealth, but about creating a life of financial security and fulfillment. Keep in mind the ultimate purpose behind your financial goals – whether that's providing for your family, having the freedom to pursue your passions, or making a positive impact in your community. This sense of purpose can be a powerful motivator during challenging times.

It's also important to maintain a healthy perspective on money. While financial success is important, it shouldn't come at the expense of your health, relationships, or personal integrity. Strive for a balanced approach that allows you to improve your financial situation while also nurturing other important aspects of your life. Don't be afraid to seek professional advice when needed. Financial advisors, tax professionals, and other experts can provide valuable insights and help you make more informed decisions. While it's important to educate yourself about personal finance, recognizing when you need expert guidance is a smart financial decision in itself. Stay vigilant against lifestyle inflation as your income grows. It's natural to want to improve your standard of living as you earn more, but maintaining some level of frugality can significantly accelerate your progress towards financial goals. Before increasing your spending in response to increased income, consider how you might use that additional money to fast-track your financial objectives. Cultivate a mindset of abundance rather than scarcity. While it's important to be mindful of your spending and saving, constantly focusing on what you lack can lead to stress and poor financial decisions. Instead, practice gratitude for what you have and approach your finances from a perspective of opportunity and growth. Remember that comparison is the thief of joy – especially when it comes to finances. In the age of social media, it's easy to fall into the trap of comparing your financial situation to others. However, these comparisons are often based on incomplete information and can lead to discouragement or unwise financial decisions. Focus on your own progress and goals rather than measuring yourself against others.

Consider the power of giving in your financial plan. Whether through charitable donations or helping friends and family, the act of giving can provide a sense of purpose and perspective to your financial journey. Many financially successful individuals find that giving becomes an increasingly important and fulfilling aspect of their financial lives as their wealth grows. Stay informed about economic trends and how they might impact your financial situation, but avoid making knee-jerk reactions to short-term market fluctuations or economic news. A long-term perspective is crucial for making smart financial decisions and avoiding costly mistakes based on temporary conditions. Remember that financial success is not just about the end result, but about the person you become in the process. The discipline, patience, and wisdom you develop on your financial journey are valuable in all areas of life. Embrace the learning process and the personal growth that comes with managing your finances effectively. Consider sharing your financial knowledge and experiences with others, particularly younger generations. Teaching others about personal finance not only helps them but can also reinforce your own understanding and commitment to sound financial principles. Stay curious and open to new ideas and opportunities. The financial world is constantly evolving, and maintaining a mindset of curiosity can help you adapt to new circumstances and take advantage of emerging opportunities.

Finally, remember that the ultimate goal of financial success is to create a life of security, freedom, and fulfillment. Keep this bigger picture in mind as you make daily financial decisions. Each choice you make is an opportunity to move closer to the life you envision for yourself. In conclusion, staying motivated and making smart financial decisions is an ongoing process that requires commitment, patience, and perseverance. By keeping your goals in mind, celebrating small victories, learning from setbacks, staying educated, and maintaining a balanced perspective, you can navigate your financial journey successfully. Remember that every financial decision you make is an opportunity to improve your financial future. Stay committed to your goals, trust in the process, and believe in your ability to create the financial life you desire. Your future self will thank you for the smart decisions you make today. Here's to your continued financial success and the exciting journey ahead!

GLOSSARY

Glossary of Financial Terms

401(k): A tax-advantaged retirement savings plan sponsored by an employer.

Annuity: A financial product that pays out a fixed stream of payments to an individual.

Asset: Anything of value that can be converted into cash.

Asset Allocation: The process of dividing investments among different kinds of assets, such as stocks, bonds, and cash.

Bear Market: A market condition in which the prices of securities are falling, and widespread pessimism causes the negative sentiment to be self-sustaining.

Bond: A fixed income investment in which an investor loans money to an entity (typically corporate or governmental) which borrows the funds for a defined period of time at a fixed interest rate.

Bull Market: A market condition in which prices are rising or are expected to rise.

Capital Gain: The profit earned on the sale of an asset like stocks, bonds, or real estate.

Compound Interest: Interest calculated on the initial principal and also on the accumulated interest of previous periods.

Credit Score: A numerical expression based on a level analysis of a person's credit files, to represent the creditworthiness of an individual.

Debt-to-Income Ratio: A personal finance measure that compares an individual's debt payment to his or her overall income.

Diversification: A risk management technique that mixes a wide variety of investments within a portfolio.

Dividend: A distribution of a portion of a company's earnings, decided by the board of directors, to a class of its shareholders.

Emergency Fund: Money set aside for unexpected expenses or financial emergencies.

ETF (Exchange-Traded Fund): A marketable security that tracks an index, a commodity, bonds, or a basket of assets like an index fund.

FICO Score: A type of credit score that makes up a substantial portion of the credit report that lenders use to assess an applicant's credit risk.

Fixed Income: A type of investing or budgeting style that provides a steady stream of income.

IRA (Individual Retirement Account): A tax-advantaged investing tool for individuals to earmark funds for retirement savings.

Inflation: A general increase in prices and fall in the purchasing value of money.

Liability: A company's legal debts or obligations that arise during the course of business operations.

Liquidity: The degree to which an asset or security can be quickly bought or sold in the market without affecting the asset's price.

Market Capitalization: The total dollar market value of a company's outstanding shares.

Mutual Fund: An investment vehicle made up of a pool of funds collected from many investors for the purpose of investing in securities such as stocks, bonds, money market instruments and similar assets.

Net Worth: The value of all assets, minus the total of all liabilities.

Portfolio: A grouping of financial assets such as stocks, bonds, commodities, currencies and cash equivalents, as well as their fund counterparts.

Risk Tolerance: The degree of variability in investment returns that an individual is willing to withstand.

Roth IRA: An individual retirement account that offers tax-free growth and tax-free withdrawals in retirement.

Stock: A type of security that signifies ownership in a corporation and represents a claim on part of the corporation's assets and earnings.

Tax Deduction: A reduction in taxable income for a taxpayer.

Volatility: A statistical measure of the dispersion of returns for a given security or market index.

Yield: The income return on an investment, such as the interest or dividends received from holding a particular security.

RECOMMENDED RESOURCES FOR TEENS

As you embark on your journey to financial literacy and success, it's crucial to have access to reliable, engaging, and age-appropriate resources. Here's a curated list of books, websites, and apps that can help you expand your financial knowledge and develop good money habits.

Books

1. "The Teenager's Guide to Money" by Jonathan Self

   This book offers practical advice on earning, saving, and spending money wisely, tailored specifically for teenagers.

2. "Rich Dad Poor Dad for Teens" by Robert Kiyosaki

   A teen-friendly version of the bestselling personal finance book, it introduces concepts like assets and liabilities in an accessible way.

3. "The Simple Path to Wealth" by JL Collins

   While not exclusively for teens, this book provides clear, straightforward advice on investing and building long-term wealth.

4. "Why Didn't They Teach Me This in School?" by Cary Siegel

   This book covers 99 personal money management principles, offering practical lessons often overlooked in formal education.

5. "The Motley Fool Investment Guide for Teens" by David and Tom Gardner

   Written by the founders of The Motley Fool, this book introduces teens to the world of investing with humor and clarity.

6. "Teen Entrepreneur Toolbox" by Anthony ONeal

   This resource is perfect for teens interested in starting their own business, offering practical guidance and motivation.

7. "How to Money: Your Ultimate Visual Guide to the Basics of Finance" by Jean Chatzky and Kathryn Tuggle

   This visually appealing book breaks down complex financial concepts into easily digestible pieces.

Websites

1. Investopedia (www.investopedia.com)

   While not exclusively for teens, Investopedia offers a wealth of information on financial terms and concepts, including a specific section for young adults.

2. Banzai (www.teachbanzai.com)

   This financial literacy program offers free courses and real-life scenarios to help teens understand personal finance.

3. Practical Money Skills (www.practicalmoneyskills.com)

   Visa's financial literacy website includes games, calculators, and lesson plans for teens to learn about money management.

4. Next Gen Personal Finance (www.ngpf.org)

   This non-profit organization provides free personal finance curriculum and resources for students and educators.

5. Teens Got Cents (www.teensgotcents.com)

   Created by a teen for teens, this website offers advice on saving money, making money, and living frugally.

6. Young Americans Center for Financial Education (www.yacenter.org)

   This organization offers programs, classes, and resources to help young people develop strong financial habits.

7. Khan Academy - Personal Finance (www.khanacademy.org/college-careers-more/personal-finance)

   This free online learning platform offers courses on various personal finance topics, suitable for teens and adults alike.

Apps

1. Mint

   While primarily for adults, Mint can be a great tool for teens to start tracking their spending and creating budgets. It provides a comprehensive overview of financial accounts and spending patterns.

2. FamZoo

   This app helps parents teach kids about money management through virtual family banks, prepaid cards, and chore charts.

3. Greenlight

   A debit card and app designed for kids and teens, allowing parents to monitor spending and set controls while giving teens hands-on money management experience.

4. Acorns

   An investing app that rounds up purchases to the nearest dollar and invests the difference. It's a great way for teens to start investing with small amounts.

5. Toshl Finance

   A budgeting app with a fun, colorful interface that makes tracking expenses engaging for teens.

6. RoosterMoney

   This app helps younger teens track their allowance, set savings goals, and learn about responsible spending.

7. Zogo

   A gamified financial literacy app that rewards learning with gift cards, making financial education fun and engaging for teens.

Additional Resources

1. Junior Achievement (www.juniorachievement.org)

   This organization offers programs and resources to educate students about workforce readiness, entrepreneurship, and financial literacy.

2. Stock Market Game (www.stockmarketgame.org)

   An online simulation of the global capital markets that engages students in grades 4-12 in the world of investing.

3. H&R Block Budget Challenge (www.hrblock.com/budget-challenge/)

   A free teen financial literacy program that replicates real-world budgeting and personal finance decision-making.

4. Federal Reserve Education (www.federalreserveeducation.org)

   Offers free educational resources about economics and personal finance for students and educators.

5. MyMoney.gov (www.mymoney.gov)

   A U.S. government website dedicated to teaching Americans the basics of financial education.

Remember, the key to financial literacy is not just reading or using these resources, but actively applying the knowledge to your own life. Start small by creating a budget, tracking your expenses, or setting savings goals. As you grow more comfortable with these basic concepts, you can explore more advanced topics like investing and long-term financial planning.

Don't be afraid to discuss what you're learning with your parents, teachers, or other trusted adults. They can provide valuable insights and help you apply these concepts to your specific situation. Financial education is a lifelong journey, and these resources are just the beginning. Stay curious, keep learning, and you'll be well on your way to financial success.

FINAL QUIZ

Welcome to the final section of our book! This comprehensive quiz is designed to test your understanding of the key financial concepts we've covered throughout this journey. Don't worry if you don't know all the answers - this quiz is meant to be a learning tool, helping you identify areas where you might need to revisit or study further. Good luck!

Section 1: Basic Financial Concepts

1. What is the difference between a need and a want in budgeting?

a) Needs are essential for survival, wants are desirable but not necessary
b) Needs are expensive, wants are cheap
c) Needs are recurring expenses, wants are one-time purchases
d) There is no difference, they are interchangeable terms

2. What does the term "pay yourself first" mean?

a) Always treat yourself to something nice before paying bills
b) Prioritize saving a portion of your income before spending on other things
c) Pay off your debts before spending on anything else
d) Invest in yourself through education before saving money

3. What is compound interest?

a) Interest paid only on the principal amount
b) Interest paid on both the principal and accumulated interest
c) A type of loan with very high interest rates
d) Interest that compounds only once a year

4. What is the purpose of an emergency fund?

a) To save for retirement
b) To cover unexpected expenses or financial emergencies
c) To invest in the stock market
d) To pay for regular monthly bills

5. What is a credit score?

a) The total amount of debt you owe
b) Your monthly income
c) A numerical representation of your creditworthiness
d) The interest rate on your credit card

Section 2: Budgeting and Saving

6. Which of the following is NOT typically considered a fixed expense?

a) Rent or mortgage payment
b) Car insurance premium
c) Grocery bill
d) Student loan payment

7. What is the 50/30/20 budgeting rule?

a) Save 50%, spend 30% on needs, and 20% on wants
b) Spend 50% on needs, 30% on wants, and save 20%
c) Invest 50%, save 30%, and spend 20%
d) Pay 50% in taxes, save 30%, and spend 20%

8. Which of the following is generally considered the LEAST liquid asset?

a) Cash in a savings account
b) Stocks in a brokerage account
c) Real estate property
d) Money market funds

9. What is the primary benefit of creating a budget?

a) It automatically increases your income
b) It eliminates all your expenses
c) It helps you understand and control your spending
d) It guarantees you'll never go into debt

10. What is the first step in creating a budget?

a) Cutting all unnecessary expenses
b) Opening a new bank account
c) Tracking your income and expenses
d) Setting financial goals

Section 3: Debt and Credit

11. What is the difference between a credit card and a debit card?

a) Credit cards are plastic, debit cards are metal
b) Credit cards borrow money from the issuer, debit cards use your own money
c) Credit cards can only be used online, debit cards only in stores
d) There is no difference, they are the same thing

12. What is the debt snowball method?

a) Paying off the largest debt first
b) Paying off the debt with the highest interest rate first
c) Paying off the smallest debt first, then moving to the next smallest
d) Making minimum payments on all debts

13. What factor typically has the largest impact on your credit score?

a) Your income
b) Your education level
c) Your payment history
d) The number of credit cards you have

14. What is a secured credit card?

a) A card that requires a PIN for every purchase
b) A card that is backed by a cash deposit
c) A card with the highest credit limit
d) A card that can only be used for online purchases

15. What is the main purpose of a credit report?

a) To show your bank account balance
b) To list your assets and liabilities
c) To provide a history of your credit and debt management
d) To determine your tax bracket

Section 4: Investing and Retirement Planning

16. What is diversification in investing?

a) Investing all your money in one promising stock
b) Spreading investments across various asset classes to reduce risk
c) Changing your investment strategy every month
d) Only investing in foreign markets

17. What is the difference between a traditional IRA and a Roth IRA?

a) Traditional IRA contributions are tax-deductible now, Roth IRA withdrawals are tax-free in retirement
b) Traditional IRA is for employees, Roth IRA is for self-employed individuals
c) Traditional IRA can only invest in stocks, Roth IRA can invest in bonds
d) There is no difference, they are the same thing

18. What is a mutual fund?

a) A loan given by a bank to multiple borrowers
b) A savings account shared by family members
c) A pool of money from many investors used to purchase a diversified portfolio of securities
d) A government program to fund public projects

19. What does "buy low, sell high" mean in investing?

a) Always buy stocks on Monday and sell on Friday
b) Purchase investments when prices are low and sell when prices have increased
c) Only invest in low-risk, high-return opportunities
d) Buy expensive stocks and sell cheap ones

20. What is the primary advantage of starting to save for retirement early?

a) You can retire at any age you want
b) You'll never have to worry about money again
c) You benefit from compound interest over a longer period
d) You can stop saving once you reach a certain age

Section 5: Insurance and Risk Management

21. What is the purpose of insurance?

a) To make you wealthy
b) To protect against financial losses from unexpected events
c) To avoid paying taxes
d) To increase your credit score

22. What type of insurance covers damage to your car from an accident?

a) Liability insurance

b) Comprehensive insurance

c) Collision insurance

d) Life insurance

23. What is a deductible in insurance?

a) The monthly premium you pay

b) The maximum amount the insurance will pay

c) The amount you pay out-of-pocket before insurance coverage kicks in

d) The discount you get for being a safe driver

24. What does term life insurance provide?

a) Coverage for a specified period of time

b) Coverage for your entire life

c) Coverage for property damage

d) Coverage for medical expenses

25. What is the purpose of disability insurance?

a) To replace income if you're unable to work due to illness or injury

b) To pay for damage to your home

c) To cover funeral expenses

d) To protect against lawsuits

Section 6: Taxes and Financial Planning

26. What is the difference between a tax deduction and a tax credit?

a) A deduction reduces taxable income, a credit reduces tax owed directly

b) A deduction is for businesses, a credit is for individuals

c) A deduction increases your refund, a credit decreases it

d) There is no difference, they are the same thing

27. What is a 1040 form?

a) A form to apply for a loan
b) A form to open a bank account
c) The standard form for filing individual income tax returns
d) A form to claim unemployment benefits

28. What is the purpose of a W-4 form?

a) To report your annual income to the IRS
b) To apply for a credit card
c) To tell your employer how much tax to withhold from your paycheck
d) To file your tax return

29. What is capital gains tax?

a) Tax on your salary
b) Tax on profits from selling investments
c) Tax on your savings account interest
d) Tax on gifts you receive

30. What is the benefit of a 529 plan?

a) It provides health insurance for children
b) It offers tax advantages for saving for education expenses
c) It's a type of retirement account
d) It protects against identity theft

Section 7: Financial Responsibility and Ethics

31. What is identity theft?

a) Forgetting your own name
b) Using someone else's personal information for financial gain
c) Changing your name legally
d) Sharing your social security number with family members

32. What is a Ponzi scheme?

a) A legitimate investment strategy

b) A type of insurance policy

c) A fraudulent investment scam promising high returns with little risk

d) A method for balancing your budget

33. What is the purpose of the Securities and Exchange Commission (SEC)?

a) To set interest rates for loans

b) To regulate the stock market and protect investors

c) To print money

d) To collect taxes

34. What is insider trading?

a) Buying and selling stocks within your own company

b) Trading stocks based on material, non-public information

c) Investing in foreign markets

d) Daytrading stocks frequently

35. What is a fiduciary duty in finance?

a) The obligation to act in the best interest of another party

b) The duty to maximize profits at any cost

c) The responsibility to pay taxes on time

d) The requirement to have insurance

Congratulations on completing the quiz! Remember, the goal is not just to get the right answers, but to understand the concepts behind them. If you struggled with any sections, don't worry - use this as an opportunity to revisit those topics in the book. Financial literacy is a lifelong journey, and this quiz is just one step in that process.

Made in United States
Troutdale, OR
12/11/2024